MAKING THE BEST OF IT

How to Cope With Being Handicapped

MAKING THE BEST OF IT

How to Cope With Being Handicapped

GILLIAN K. HOLZHAUSER

A Ballantine/Epiphany Book
Ballantine Books · New York

Library of Congress Cataloging-in-Publication Data

Holzhauser, Gillian K., 1955–
  Making the best of it—how to cope with being handicapped.

  "A Ballantine/Epiphany book."
  1. Physically handicapped—Psychology. I. Title.
HV3011.H65 1986   155.9′16   85-26829
ISBN 0-345-33116-8

Design by Holly Johnson
Manufactured in the United States of America

First Edition: June 1986
10 9 8 7 6 5 4 3 2 1

Acknowledgments

Any author knows that it is not by his or her effort alone that a book is written. *Making the Best of It* is no exception. My deepest appreciation to Constance Tallman and Kathleen Crates for their suggestions and encouragement all along the way.

To my father, Dr. E. K. Holzhauser, for his unwavering enthusiasm directed toward this book.

But most of all to my friend Robert L. Brummel, who knows just when to stimulate a new idea, steady a wavering hand or touch a faltering spirit.

Contents

Introduction

The opinions and views expressed within the pages of this book come primarily from the experiences of the author. Since she has been legally blind from the age of five months, her perspective is based, in general, on physical handicaps, and specifically on visual handicaps. However, it is believed that many of the same problems, frustrations, and triumphs are experienced by those who are handicapped in other ways. Even more important, the solutions that she offers are useful regardless of the specific nature of a person's handicap. In fact, the solutions are beneficial to anyone with a handicap that affects body, mind, or spirit.

Foreword

I have no idea of the number of handicapped people in this country, but every one of them would, I believe, derive real benefit from Gillian K. Holzhauser's book *Making the Best of It: How to Cope With Being Handicapped.*

Why may I be so certain of this book? Because while personally I am not handicapped physically in any sense, still I found myself being helped as I read the manuscript. It could be we are all handicapped in one way or another, if not physically, perhaps in spirit or emotionally or in our thought processes. Reading the book I found myself thinking how sound a philosopher Gillian is, and a wise student of human emotions and psychology, too. I seemed to draw peace from her peace, strength from her strength, deepened faith from her obviously sturdy and reasoned faith.

While Gillian discusses the anger that may well up in a handicapped person at his plight, she surmounted her own anger and indeed gained victory over the bruised emotions one who is handicapped is bound to suffer. There is a quiet serenity, indeed a sweetness of disposition, that comes through in this book, and that despite the shackles of legal blindness this extraordinarily capable young woman has faced. Even when told that her sight would never improve and the intense anguish of hopelessness engulfed her spirit, she struggled to right herself.

By sound thinking and spiritual insight she was able to look forward always toward a bright future. The great Samuel Johnson used to say, "It's worth a thousand pounds to have a bright point of view." I'd say it is worth much more than that, especially when you achieve it through darkness. In reading this book one will find how to be a winner, an achiever, an overcomer, how to get on top of life's handicaps and stay there.

All of us have heard people ask in moments of sorrow, suffering, or bitterness, "Why did God let this happen to me?" The query is as old as the human race, and many have tried more or less effectively to deal with it. This question is handled by Gillian Holzhauser in a thoughtful, meaningful, and, I believe, satisfying way. But she had to hammer out her deep philosophy of "why" on the anvil of heartache.

Actually, this book is a great human document written by a young woman who is handicapped by blindness but whom God compensated for her sightlessness by the gift of insight. And she was given the ability to feel the pain of all handicapped persons and the compassion to understand and the writing ability to communicate courage. But above all, she developed the power of faith to help them to triumph as she has triumphed.

I commend this fine book to all people who are handicapped physically and to others who are no less handicapped in more subtle ways. The book will help anyone who needs help. And who doesn't?

Norman Vincent Peale

ONE

What Does It Really Mean?

Handicapped. **What does** the word bring to mind? A person in a wheelchair making his way down a corridor? Someone on crutches whose pant leg dangles limply below the knee? To be sure, these are examples of handicaps, but what does the word *really* mean?

The dictionary suggests, "a disadvantage that makes achievement unusually difficult." Within that definition there are countless variations depending upon the viewpoint of the person using the word. A parent might add "and may put a strain on family living." A teacher might add "and that poses extra challenges as the student tries to learn."

Few of us who are handicapped can forget the first time the stark reality hit home for us that we were *truly handicapped*. In kindergarten I can remember playing outside at recess. An older boy who was known as the school bully came up behind me and said, "Gee, your glasses are thick! You look even worse than me." With that he gave me a shove that sent me reeling to the ground. Despite the teacher's efforts to comfort me and her stern reprimand to the boy, I knew from that moment on that I *was* different from most of the other kids. My sight was poor. My glasses were thick. In short, I was handicapped.

You must decide for yourself what the word *handicapped* means to you. Don't let anyone else, however well-meaning he or she may be, make that decision for you. You may say, "I don't have to define it. I live with it every day. I *know* what it means to be handicapped." But the truth is that you *do* need to take a good hard look at your own personal viewpoint. To a great extent, that will determine just how successful you will be in dealing with your own circumstances and growing to be as happy and personally fulfilled as you are capable of becoming.

I recall my own reaction at first, which was to shut out the fact that I was handicapped. One day when I was about nine years old, the doorbell rang. A tall slender woman of about sixty was at the door, carrying a large supply of oversize books. "Are you Gillian?" she asked. When I nodded, she said, "These are for you. They're books with big letters and they can help you read better."

"What do I need those for?" I asked politely, though I was unable to conceal my irritation. Before she could answer, I went on. "I get along fine with my own books. Why don't you take them to someone who really needs them?" The woman left in considerable bewilderment.

When I told my dad about the experience, he said, "Those books help people like you who don't see so well to read better. They're specially made with the large print that you need."

"Not for me, they aren't. I sent the woman packing!" If my father was irritated with me, he did not show it, and he made no further attempt to educate me on the specifics of my condition. Of course, in truth, I *did* have problems reading regular-size print. It was necessary for me to hold a book within a few inches of my face to read it. But to my way of thinking, that was better than accepting the fact that I could have benefitted from large-print books.

How you view the term *handicapped*, and, more important, how you view your own handicap, will determine to a large degree the response you get from other people. This raises an important point! Your handicap is a part of you. In much the same way as the color of your hair, your height, and other distinguishing characteristics make up the person you are, so too does your handicap. You cannot deny that fact.

But your handicap is only *one* part of what you are. The way you view your handicap may, however, affect many of your other characteristics. An old-fashioned example helps to illustrate this point. A glass sits on the table with water in it, but filled only halfway. Is that glass half empty or is it half full? The answer will depend on you!

Thus, when I am introduced to someone, I would not say, "Hi! I'm Gillian Holzhauser. I'm legally blind." On the other hand, when applying for a job or involved in another activity where knowledge of my handicap would be helpful to someone else, I would not hide the fact. On the contrary, I bring up the subject, because if I am the one who raises it, then my attitude toward it will be immediately apparent. The other person can see and feel my reaction, which will help him decide how he will respond to me.

In junior high school, I was interested in being chosen as a student librarian for the year. The teacher who interviewed me asked a number of routine questions and then said, "You have trouble seeing, don't you? Do you think that would be a problem?"

"Yes, I do." I said. "But I have learned to live with my sight problem quite well. If I need extra help, I can always ask for it. Otherwise, I'd like to be treated just like all the other students who work in the library."

Apparently, I convinced the librarian that while my sight problem might pose some special difficulty at times, ordinarily it would not interfere with the work expected of me, and moreover, that I would let the librarian know when I was having difficulty. Then she would not be responsible for constantly overseeing my work or wondering how I was getting along.

I *was* one of the students selected, which proved to me that I could influence the way people viewed my problem. My words and my actions helped to overcome the stigma often attached to visually impaired persons.

If you are in doubt about how significant your handicap is to you, ask yourself this question: "When I think about myself, what do I think of first?" If you answer "the fact that I am handicapped" (or "the fact that I cannot see" or whatever your specific handicap is), then that is a pretty fair indication that you view this as the most important facet of your total self.

You need to know that perceiving your handicap as important does not necessarily mean that you have an unhealthy attitude. However, it *does* mean that you must be clear about how you look at this part of your life, because your future depends on it.

The next question to ask is "Aside from my handicap, what other characteristics are significant about me?" If you have difficulty responding to this question, then it is a virtual certainty that you have allowed the fact that you are handicapped to cloud your thinking about the abilities, likes, dislikes, and beliefs that combine to make you the person you are. If you can respond to the question but the list you prepare in your mind is a short one, then you still have work to do. For while you have started to look at yourself as a composite being, you are still growing in that knowledge and need to expand your list.

Another good exercise to help you put the word *handicapped* in perspective is to ask several close friends to describe you. Tell them to use any words they wish, to include negative as well as positive characteristics. Remind them that they need not spare your feelings, because for the exercise to be effective you must have their honest assessment. As you listen, see how long it takes for the fact that you are handicapped to be mentioned. This may tell you a great deal. Your handicap may be more or, probably, less of an issue than you first thought.

Any or all of these short exercises will help you to understand the word *handicapped* on your own terms. It will then be much easier and much more rewarding for you to delve into the problems that your handicap creates. And there *are* problems.

As we shall see in the following chapters, these problems take various forms. How significant each of these problem areas is in your life depends upon you. Yet what is equally apparent is that there are also solutions, and these too will be explored. Out of this exploration should ultimately come a more objective, healthier way for you to live with your handicap, without letting it become "an albatross around your neck."

TWO

The Physical Problems

The physical problems of a handicapped person fall basically into two categories. One category is the handicapping condition itself, such as loss of hearing, loss of sight, or the absence of a limb. The second category consists of the problems that are the indirect result of the handicap. For example, in some victims of hearing loss there is a definite tendency toward impaired speech. The primary handicap is the inability to hear well. A resulting physical problem is poor articulation due to the inability to hear sounds correctly.

Regardless of which type of physical problem you have, the method of dealing with it is similar. First and foremost, learn all you can about your handicap. There is nothing worse than being a victim of your own ignorance. For that is the seed from which fear, anxiety, and other undesirable feelings can grow. Once these feelings have become a part of your life, they can fester and multiply until they overrun your mind much as an untended garden becomes overgrown with weeds. It is far harder to rid oneself of these weeds than to prevent or minimize their presence in the first place.

"All well and good," you may say. "But I am not a doctor. All those ten-dollar words are like Greek to me. How can I learn what I need to know about my physical problems?" This is a natural reaction, for few people enjoy delving into medical problems—especially those that affect them directly. But, like coming to grips with your own definition of your handicap, this is an essential step if you are to become involved in the challenge of helping yourself!

Begin your learning process by asking the questions that are uppermost in your mind. Organize your thoughts. Perhaps the best method of ensuring good organization is to prepare a notebook to be used exclusively for items pertaining to your handicap. Make a list of your questions in one section of the notebook. Leave ample space below each question for the answer. This will prevent your becoming confused by jumbled notes when you review the responses at a later time.

By far, the best person to consult is the medical professional (usually a physician) who is treating you, for he or she knows your condition and all its facets better than anyone else. This is especially true if he has been handling your case for a substantial length of time. However, remember that his time is limited. Physicians are on a tight schedule; usually their waiting rooms are crowded with patients. This is precisely the reason why your list of questions becomes so valuable. Take time in preparing it. Start it one day; mull it over the next day, adding to it or deleting from it as needed. Try to group questions dealing with the same general subject area together. For example, if you want to know about the medication you take, the amount of physical activity that is recommended for you, or the proper diet you should follow, make it a major topic area. Underneath, list the specific questions that you have. Under the Medication heading, for example, you might want to explore possible side effects or the length of time the doctor expects you to be on the medication. Under the Physical Activity heading, you may want to ask about specific sports you enjoy and how they could be modified to fit your limitations.

Two words of caution should be inserted here. First of all, when you ask questions, you undoubtedly will get answers. While that may seem to be readily apparent, take another look. In some cases, the answers you get will be what you wanted to hear. But on other topics the physician may suggest limitations or may make other comments that are not to your liking. Remember that you are seeking the greatest amount of knowledge he can impart to you—whether you like its content or not. Think how much better it is to have honest answers than to be plagued by uncertainty and doubt.

Second, it will not always be possible for your physician to answer your questions, because he may not know just how to respond. A good physician will admit this readily. He will either offer to find out the information you are seeking or admit that there is no specific way to reply to your query. If there is no specific answer he can give you, accept this. Be grateful for what information *is* available and utilize it to its fullest extent.

Continue your learning process by asking your doctor for any materials he might recommend for you to read. Reading is something that you can do on your own time and at your own pace. You may then ask him questions at some future appointment based upon what you have read. In addition to giving you more information, this will also demonstrate to your doctor that you are willing and eager to learn whatever you can as a start toward playing a more vital role in your own treatment process. Without a doubt, your physician will be impressed and pleased that you are trying to help yourself!

Another word of caution is advisable here. As you read about your handicap and about other persons who are likewise afflicted, remember that no two people are exactly alike. Each handicapping condition will vary slightly from yours. Maybe the person was at a different stage of life when first experiencing the problem. Perhaps the individual has additional health problems that you do not have. In any event, every case is a little different. If as you read you are in doubt as to whether a specific characteristic applies to you, jot it down in a special section of your notebook reserved for this purpose. Then discuss it with your doctor at your next appointment.

Now that you are beginning to gain valuable factual knowledge about your handicap, remember that this is an ongoing process. You will not accomplish it overnight. Read anything and everything that is available to you.

Once you have gained insight into your physical condition, be ready to accept the fact that there may be some things you simply cannot do. When you know that this is the case (either because your doctor has told you so or because you have actually tried it), be mature enough to accept it.

The need for this maturity was brought home to me at the age of sixteen when all of my friends obtained their driver's licenses. More than anything else, I wanted to be able to drive a car too. Peer pressure and a love of independence increased my eagerness.

It was not to be, however. In applying for a temporary license, I was asked to take a vision test. The first time I flunked it entirely. The second time I barely passed and was restricted to "daylight hours only." Then began a series of driving instructors and a large outlay of funds. I would approach lesson after lesson with renewed hope—only to return home discouraged and angry. Finally, I had to come to the conclusion that I simply did not have the vision or the coordination to drive.

For days afterward I was in a depressed state of mind. My whole world had collapsed. I was destined to a life of dependence and limited activity. Eventually, a trusted friend could tolerate it no longer. "You don't realize how lucky you are," she said with more emotion than tact. "You're so busy feeling sorry for yourself that you haven't stopped to think that your efforts were thwarted before you injured yourself or someone else. What's more, your family and friends know that you have tried and admire you for it. They will help you all they can. But it's up to you to show all of us that you have the maturity to accept what has happened to you like an adult!"

My depression did not disappear overnight, nor did my realization of the truth come without some additional pain. But gradually, in my heart as well as in my head, I realized that she was right. How each of us handles the situations that confront us is the true indication of our maturity and adulthood.

Aside from those activities that may be completely out of the question for you, your physical limitations may prompt you to do some things differently from other people. This is the exciting part! It is here that your initiative and creativity are put to the ultimate test. You take the traditional way of accomplishing a given task and then adapt it to your specialized needs. For example, as a young adult I became keenly aware of my need for exercise. I knew that many people gained their exercise from bicycling. But I was also aware that I have a poor sense of balance and because of it could not ride a two-wheeler even as a youngster.

What could I do? Give up the idea of this type of exercise? No, there was a better solution. Instead, I bought an adult tri-wheeler cycle. Understandably, I received my share of stares. One woman passing me on the sidewalk even said, "Aren't you a little old to be riding a tricycle, lady?" But the negative aspects of my new endeavor were minimal in comparison to the satisfaction I derived from having found a safe, enjoyable mode of exercise.

A few years later I added a new dimension to my cycling by purchasing a stationary bicycle with a steadying bar across the back. Again, I gained the sensation of biking, but in this case felt even less chance of impending danger. In the comfort of my own basement I can pedal for as long as I wish, all the while observing the odometer as the miles mount.

Sometimes it may be necessary to find replacement activities for those things that are not possible for you to do. This is especially true with hobbies. If you are unable to be a bowler, take up Scrabble instead. If you cannot jog, turn to hiking as an alternative. Far more important than the specific sport is that you find a sport, any sport, that you are able to engage in and enjoy.

Finally, be cognizant of the fact that the physical activities that you are able to handle effectively may change over time. You may be able to do something a year from now that you are unable to do at present. Of course, the opposite situation is also a possibility. Enjoy what you can at the present time. Do not look back to yesterday or anticipate the possibilities of tomorrow. Instead, live today!

THREE

The Mental Problems

"Mind over matter." You have probably heard or even used that expression yourself. It indicates that what our mind believes, how our mind reasons, is indeed a powerful influence over the way we behave, even over the manner in which we live. This leads to one of the greatest problems of being handicapped—a poor self-image. In our minds we see ourselves as being inferior, deficient, and unable to meet the challenges of daily living.

A personal experience will help to illustrate

the very destructive nature of these poor self-images. In the elementary grades it was necessary for me to walk down a rather steep incline to get to school each morning. During the first winter that I walked to school alone, this incline soon became covered with a thick layer of ice and a fine layer of powdery snow on top. One morning as I approached this spot I had a vision of myself falling to the ground as I attempted to make my way down the incline. Sure enough, when I got there I tumbled to the ground, my schoolbooks flying in every direction. To make matters worse, an important homework paper was ruined as it fell out from between the pages of one of my books and landed in the snow. From that day on, each time I would approach that spot a surge of fear would run through my body. Even during spring and fall months, in my mind I fell over that incline ten, fifty, a hundred times.

While one such experience will not create a negative self-concept on its own, a group of these experiences undoubtedly will. When this happens, you are fighting a double handicap—your initial disability plus that of a poor self-concept. What is more, a poor self-concept is far more devastating and far more destructive than your disability—whatever that is—could ever be. For there is in such cases what I like to call "a spillover effect." When you imagine yourself as incapable of accomplishing a specific task or coping with a certain problem, you have already put into motion all the ingredients to formulate a negative self-image. The next time it is just that much easier, when faced with a similar task, to imagine that you cannot do it, that it is "beyond you."

People, handicapped or not, have denied themselves more opportunities and declined more challenges because of a negative self-concept than for any other single reason.

Another problem is the fear of failure. As human beings we are taught to admire the successful. The articles we read, the television shows we see, often deal with success—a company's top salesman, baseball's most valuable player, the valedictorian of a high school class. These are in themselves positive images. But when we look at our own lives, can we picture ourselves achieving a similar kind of success? Or instead do we say, "Well, that's wonderful for him or her. But that's not for me. I couldn't do it."

When we are afraid of failing, we are denying that we are entitled to make mistakes. Though it is difficult, we must remember that everyone makes mistakes at some point. Are we any different?

A teacher I knew told an all-A student that she thought it would be good for him to get a B in a subject one term. The young man, enraged at someone whom he had previously considered his "favorite" teacher, fumed, "How can you say that? Don't you want me to succeed?" The teacher, in her wisdom, responded, "It is precisely because I want you to succeed that I hope you will receive a B sometime. You would look upon that as having failed, having let your parents down. But I see that as letting yourself know that you are not always perfect, that sometimes you will fall short of perfection."

It is important also to note that those who are afraid of failing put themselves under a tremendous amount of stress. They often exert superhuman effort in quest of continued success and make many sacrifices—not the least of which is peace of mind—in the process. Chronic worriers often miss much of what life has to offer because they are so busy worrying about whether or not they have succeeded.

A healthy self-concept, then, is the desire to do well combined with the realization that we may not always succeed. With this in mind we are ready to meet challenges as they arise rather than shying away from them in fear. When we are not successful, when we fall down, in a manner of speaking, we will get up, brush ourselves off, walk on, and seize the next opportunity that comes our way!

Another problem experienced by us as handicapped persons is the tendency to make comparisons between ourselves and others. When we make such a comparison it is frequently out of balance from the start. The reason for this is that we will compare ourselves with the other person in only one or two specific areas. Say, for example, that you have a friend who has a good sense of humor and a nice smile. These two attributes may be ones that you do not have or ones that you believe need to be improved in your particular case. You "stack up" negatively in comparison. However, if you would have compared yourself and the same friend in three or four other areas, you would very likely have found that you have other attributes which he does not have. In other words, a balance would be achieved between your positive and your negative traits, and the same thing could be said about the characteristics of your friend.

When I was in junior high school, I met a girl one day who I thought was everything I ever wanted to be. She was tall, while I was short. She had good vision, while my vision with thick corrective lenses was far less acute than hers. To my way of thinking she was perfect. One day after school she met me on the steps and said, "Could you help me with a speech I have to write for English class? I have always admired your ability to write. And you speak so well too!"

I was dumbfounded! To begin with, I couldn't

imagine how someone as pretty as she was would pay any attention to me. What was even more amazing was that she was seeking *my* help. The ability to write and speak was something I simply took for granted. Couldn't everybody do it? Apparently not, because even the thought of it made her ill at ease. In short, she was focusing on an area in which my skills could be helpful to her. All I had ever seen was how unfavorably I compared to her in looks.

In addition to being frustrating, continual comparison of yourself with others is really a waste of time. For the time you spend making the comparison could be so much better spent working on improving yourself or in pursuing an activity that you enjoy.

The poem "Desiderata" sums it up best by saying,

If you compare yourself with others, you will become vain and bitter; for always there will be greater and lesser persons than yourself.

Still another problem that the handicapped person must battle—one, in fact, that all persons must strive to combat to some degree—is that of making excuses for something done or not done. Before we look into this problem further, however, it must be pointed out that there is a profound difference between offering an explanation and making an excuse. An explanation involves stating the reasons for a course of action you have taken. For example, if all your friends went to a football game on a cold evening and you decided not to go because you are susceptible to colds and sore throats, telling someone about your decision and its reasons is an explanation.

If, on the other hand, in the same instance you had said, "The team isn't that good anyway and I knew they wouldn't win, so I stayed home," instead of giving the real reason for your decision, you would be making an excuse. Even if your team were having a losing season that year, which might make your excuse seem plausible to some people, it is nonetheless just an excuse. It was not the true reason, but rather one that you made up in your mind to save you either from further explanations or from what you might perceive to be embarrassment.

The danger with making excuses such as that illustrated above is twofold. First, your excuses may not be as logical as you think they are. Your friends and family may begin to see through your comments and wonder what it is that you are trying to hide or cover up. And chances are, their imaginations are far more vivid than the situation itself. For that reason alone, you must approach each situation truthfully.

The other danger is an even more serious one.

After a while you may become so accustomed to the excuses you are giving to others for your actions that you will begin to lose sight of your true reasoning and feelings. You will confuse your "outer self" (the person that you try to be in front of your family and friends) with your "inner self" (the person you really are, which includes your thoughts, attitudes, and feelings). Some modern psychologists would say that this could result in an "identity crisis"—confusion within yourself as to who you are. While many cases are not as severe as that, conflicts between your "inner self" and your "outer self" most certainly will force you to make artificially induced choices as to which self you will listen to more often, the one that is truly you or the one who you believe is the more "acceptable."

It may ease your mind somewhat to know that, in general, people are far more understanding of others (and the special situations in which other people find themselves) than you might think. After all, each person has his own peculiarities. These are really just different ways of doing or looking at things. Everyone is entitled to them.

Perhaps the most debilitating problem of all is the preoccupation with what will happen in the future. Handicapped or not, many people's minds are filled with aimless pondering about the future. This is understandable in anyone, but perhaps even more so for those of us who are handicapped. After all, our lives have been plagued with discomforts and uncertainties for a long time in many cases. It is quite natural that we would wonder whether the future will be brighter.

A rather ridiculous example demonstrates this difficulty. Someone came to call on an elderly lady and invited her to go shopping and then have supper the following Saturday. "No," said she, "I must stay right here by the telephone and wait for a possible long-distance call." When her friend inquired as to whether she was expecting to hear from someone in particular on Saturday, she responded, "No, but there's always the chance, and I wouldn't want to miss a call." What she was missing, of course, was what promised to be a pleasant time of fun and companionship. She was denying herself all that because she was anticipating some vague future possibility.

Now, it is quite natural for us to do a certain amount of planning ahead for the future. We schedule a doctor's appointment two weeks hence, accept a luncheon date a week from now, make arrangements for a summer vacation. But the key word here is *planning*. Setting specific objectives and determining the best way of accomplishing them in the days ahead is planning. However, that is the very opposite of a worrisome preoccupation with what might happen in the future. For such preoccupation is usually nebulous, full of uncertainties, "what ifs," "perhapses," and "maybes."

Handicapped persons and perhaps especially

the parents of handicapped children often fall into the category of those who are preoccupied with worrying about the future. Sometimes they are so concerned about who will care for their loved one when they are no longer able, or how to pay for such care, that they fail to see and appreciate the good things in the present.

The parents of a close friend of mine were so caught up in raising the money needed to care for her after their death that they nearly neglected to see the great strides she was making toward her own self-sufficiency. As a matter of fact, both her father and mother lived to see the day when she was able to rent an apartment and care for it and herself with only limited assistance. During the years when they worried so much as to what would become of her, they were much less able to enjoy the warm, enthusiastic person that she was. No amount of regret on their part could give them back the gift of those lost years.

A good rule of thumb to combat this problem is to test your worries about the future by asking, "Is there something I can do now to lessen this worry or combat this potential problem?" If there is, fine; do it. Think it through and take any steps necessary to accomplish what is needed. But if there is nothing that can be done, or nothing that can be done at this particular point in time, then let it go. Let your mind move on to other areas of thought, especially those where present action is not only possible but advisable. Not only will that particular problem be on its way to solution, but you will experience the feeling of having done something worthwhile. You will believe that there are other ways in which you can help your loved one or yourself. That infusion of self-confidence in your abilities will enhance your skill for solving other types of problems. Thus, a positive cycle of reinforcement will have been initiated.

As a member of my high school's debate team I had difficulty in following the notes of a prepared speech. To hold the notes close enough for me to read them meant covering my face almost completely. How could I solve this problem? My solution was to memorize the speech, thus making notes of any kind unnecessary. Not only did I solve the initial problem, but in so doing I gained additional recognition from the judges, who were impressed by the content and the delivery of my remarks.

A short time later I was asked to give a speech in a different type of competition. The same technique was used with only a slight modification. The few statistics that I needed to quote were printed on a card with a bold red pencil. Thus, the method for dealing with the first such problem gave me the assurance I needed to forge ahead in a new area of endeavor.

Your mind exerts a tremendous power over

your life. Your ability to think and reason is a strong force that will work either to your benefit or to your detriment. So why not have the richer, more fulfilling life that positive "mind power" guarantees? It's *your* choice!

FOUR

The Emotional Problems

Emotional problems experienced by handicapped persons differ widely with each individual. The severity of the handicap itself and the
reactions of family and friends account largely for
this difference. However, there are certain emotional problems common to nearly everyone who
is handicapped.

Perhaps the most common problem of all is the
feeling of intense anger. Sooner or later it hits all
of us—that feeling that we want to lash out at
something, at someone who we believe, perhaps

erroneously, can be blamed for our handicap. We think, "My handicap is really awful! I hate it! I'll have to put up with it the rest of my life! Whom can I blame?" Anger, like other emotions, is a natural outgrowth of the frustration we feel at being handicapped. The danger is that we not only feel this anger but also seek ways in which to vent it. We say things that we later wish had remained unsaid.

Never had the power of an angry tongue been so evident to me as it was one day following a visit to my neurosurgeon. A kind and patient gentleman, he always set aside a time for me to discuss anything important that was on my mind. On that particular day I had asked him, "What do you really think caused the disease that left me legally blind?" "No one knows for sure, Gillian," he had told me. "But some doctors believe that having parents who are older when a baby is born has a great deal to do with it."

The doctor also added, "Of course, that is just a theory and we really don't have any answers at this point." I did not hear the last part of his explanation, however. For I had already shut out the remainder of his words. My mind could focus only on what he said about having older parents.

A short time later, when I saw my father, after barely saying hello, I lashed out at him, "Why did you have to be so old when I was born? The doctor said that's what made me handicapped. It's all *your* fault, but it's *my* life that is ruined, not yours!"

To this day I shall never forget the expression of hurt and pain that crossed my father's face. For a time he said nothing. We both just stood there. He was in shock at what I'd said; I was in shock for having said it. From the moment the words tumbled out, I regretted having said them.

After a time he simply said, "None of us can undo what we have already done, Punkin. We can only go on from here." That was the last time we ever talked about it to this very day. Yet I am sure that we both have thought of that encounter many times since.

We look for or even manufacture the slightest reason to find fault with another person. And frequently, those who we attack are the people closest to us, who love us, and whom we love more than any other people in the world. But when our anger is at its peak, we do not stop to think about our true feelings. We just want to hurt someone else the way we feel we have been hurt.

A friend who had lost his leg in a tragic accident once told me that the most important piece of equipment in his house was the punching bag in his bedroom. "It can't talk back to me," he said. "It is not logical. It cannot reason. But, most of all, I can hit it as hard as I please for as long as I please without hurting a soul." How right he was! And how perceptive he was to understand the potential for hurting others when his angry feelings exploded beyond control. While all of us do not have a punching bag or other harmless object to serve as an outlet for our rage, it is essential that we find some constructive way in which to vent the anger that is bottled up inside us.

Another friend I know says that when she is angry, she takes a long, brisk walk in the fresh air. As she is walking she lets her mind wander in any direction. Her anger is at first very strong. Gradually, however, the anger subsides and she begins to relax. The smooth, steady movement of walking calms her body and her emotions. It is not long before she has shifted gears mentally. She begins thinking less destructive thoughts, planning, instead, constructive actions that she can take to achieve better control over the cause of her anger.

Frequently, anger rules us when we believe that we have lost that all-important feeling of control over our lives. Anger reaches a fever pitch when we feel too great a degree of dependence upon others or when our repeated efforts to solve a nagging problem have failed.

By the time I was seven years old I still could not tie a shoe. Several times different members of my family attempted to teach me how, but each time they gave up, convinced that it was a skill I could not learn. In school I would leave my special gym shoes tied from one session of gym class to the next, hoping to be able to wriggle into them without untying the bow.

But one day I came home from school in tears after the shoe's bow had come untied and I was forced to limp through the remainder of that day's gym class with the untied strings dangling dangerously in every direction.

"I just have to learn how to tie!" I sobbed. "I can't stand being different anymore!" But still I did not have the hand and eye coordination to push the one string out from underneath the other to make that all-important bow. My pride was hurt, my ego bruised. Why was I so dumb?

"You're not dumb," my father tried to explain. "Your hands and eyes just don't coordinate properly."

The more I thought about those weeks of gym class yet to come before the school year ended, the angrier I became. Even when the matter was temporarily resolved by asking my seat partner to help me in exchange for sharpening her pencils with mine each morning, I still felt that painful dependence upon someone else to do something for me that I longed to be able to do for myself.

Anger is a particularly dangerous emotion, because it can come upon us from one moment to the next. Perhaps we see someone doing something we long to do or, worse yet, doing something we were once able to do but no longer can. Because of its sudden and volatile nature, anger is a feeling that must be viewed objectively *before* it strikes. It is only then that we can analyze it and have a clearer knowledge of what we must do when it hits us with all its might.

It is noteworthy that feelings of anger can be turned into something very positive. "Positive?" you ask. That's not an adjective that we usually associate with anger. But it is a possibility nonetheless. A positive result can be obtained if we take the intensity of our anger and channel it into a specific endeavor that requires all the strength and determination we can muster.

The story is told that there was a salesman who was getting his first start on a new job. Shortly thereafter the company for which he worked experienced business reverses, forcing them to lay off employees. "Last hired, first fired" was the test used to determine who should leave and so, of course, this young man was dismissed almost immediately. To say he was angry was an understatement. "I didn't even have a chance!" he moaned. But then a strange and wonderful thing happened to him. He saw an ad in a magazine for a company that offered training and a solely commission-based sales income. The young man responded and vowed that he would prove himself as a top salesman. He channeled the anger he felt toward his former employer to the most positive activity of all—proving that he was a first-class salesman. When the time came for his evaluation by the new company, he was told that his sales record far exceeded even their highest expectations. What is more, he was asked to conduct seminars for new employees, based upon his experiences. These seminars were designed to motivate the new employees to strive toward their top performance in sales. And he did! All of this arose out of a very unpleasant set of circumstances. It can even be argued that the intensity of his anger motivated him to a far greater degree than he would ever have been if he had stayed with his former employer.

A final note about anger. When we feel the sting of that emotion, however unpleasant it may be at the time, it lets us know that we are in touch with our feelings. It tells us that we care about something very deeply, that we are alive with the emotional impact of the particular situation. We are not existing in a vacuum, nor are we letting life do to us whatever it will without a reaction on our part. Take that reaction, harness it, channel it in a positive way, and the results will amaze you!

A second emotional problem, which is perhaps even more potentially destructive than anger, is guilt. Unlike anger, it does not appear in a flurry from one moment to the next but may instead germinate in our emotional being until something specific triggers it off. The seeds of guilt are usually planted when we harbor a feeling of resentment against someone for the fact that we are handicapped. At first, we want to make people pay for what we think "they" did to "us." Later, in our more rational moments, we see the senselessness of such a desire and we feel guilty for even considering it. We feel the need to blame someone for our handicap, and yet hate ourselves for blaming them.

A different source of guilt feelings comes from what we believe we have done to our loved ones—parents, siblings, spouses. A cerebral palsy victim expressed the emotion well when she told of her guilt over the time required for her therapy sessions. Her father, who had taken extensive training to give the therapy, devoted forty-five minutes three times a day to filling her therapy prescription. A business executive by profession, the man was understandably on a tight schedule, and the therapy program forced him to get up that much earlier in the morning and stay up that much later at night. His daughter's guilt over this situation became so intense that it was interfering with her sessions and impeding her progress.

One day she confided her guilt feelings to a trusted friend. The friend helped her to see that if her father did not want to take the time for the sessions or did not feel able to do so, provisions could be made for someone of equal strength and skill to take over his duties. Her friend also pointed out an aspect of this task that benefited her father. He was gone all day providing for his family's financial needs, but because of that he did not feel that he was playing an active role in his daughter's efforts toward rehabilitation and eventual independence. The physical act of manipulating her legs and other therapy routines made him feel a sense of involvement in her struggle that he would have been hard-pressed to find any other way. Thus, not only was he able to contribute to his daughter's progress, but he was also finding a positive way of working through his own emotions.

It is an undisputed fact that a handicapped person in a household can place strains and tensions upon family members that would otherwise not be present. However, feeling guilty about your handicap and dwelling upon it will not change anything. In fact, the more you think such negative thoughts, the more you are programming your mind in an unhealthy direction. Left unchecked, this programming could make such feelings begin to seem reasonable to you. Guard against this happening to you!

Instead, try taking a positive approach! Handicapped persons can bring out the very best in other people as well as in themselves. A greater degree of cooperation among family members, a greater sense of triumph when even the smallest of mountains is climbed, and a fuller sense of one's true blessings are all gifts that are within your power to give!

My sister and I went through a stage when we regretted not having a large family of aunts, uncles, and cousins. Ours was a smaller extended family, and the family we did have was widely scattered. Many were across the ocean in Europe;

others were on the West Coast. All were far away from Ohio. Our friends, on the other hand, seemed forever to be going to an aunt here, a grandmother there. One night when we sat up in bed talking as we often did after the lights were turned out, she said to me, "I wish we had all those relatives too!" She remained silent for a while, but then went on. "But when we help you, we get closer to the family we've got. Funny, isn't it?" Funny, indeed, but true nonetheless. We had managed to replace many of the satisfactions of having a large family with a sense of togetherness by uniting in a common effort. For my part, I had to fight as hard as I could to do whatever I could to combat my visual, coordination, and other problems. For their part, my sister and parents were one in their desire to see me develop to my fullest potential.

A third emotional problem that often confronts handicapped people is a feeling of hopelessness. We resign ourselves to the fact that things are really not the way we want them to be. Furthermore, we believe that another month, another year, or even several years will not make any difference in our circumstances. We give up hope for the future.

As a teenager I went through a stage of hoping that someday my vision would undergo a dramatic improvement. I had read more than my quota of magazine articles and books on foods that help the eyes, surgical cures such as cornea transplants, and exercises of all sorts that could strengthen eye muscles. I was certain that someday one or all of these methods could help me to see appreciably better. "It's only a matter of time," I told myself over and over again.

When I confided this feeling to my neurosurgeon while I was awaiting surgery, he looked at me sternly and said, "No, Gillian. That type of help is not for you. You are lucky to have any vision at all. The best you can hope for is to preserve the little bit of sight you have." I was crushed! Never be able to see any better? That thought had never entered my mind. Some day, I knew, it would be different. But now the doctor I respected more than any other contradicted my feelings of hope for a better day to come. Not only did he contradict them; he virtually destroyed them. I went home in a state of depression. No amount of effort on my part would help me to regain any part of the sight I had lost. The situation, in a word, was hopeless.

Hopelessness is much like a bottle of black ink being spilled on a white carpet. Left untreated, it will stain our emotions.

Such a feeling will affect the way we approach things today, tomorrow, every day. Regardless of what opportunity we may be given to improve our lives, if we take a "what's-the-use?" attitude, we will be none the better off for having been given the opportunity in the first place.

When this feeling of hopelessness overtakes you, do something about it immediately! Think of someone who has a more severe handicap than you have and yet is able to cope with it successfully—most of the time. You can be sure that this individual has not given up hope. Even when he suffers a setback, as every one of us inevitably does, he never loses that feeling of hope. Instead, he fights back! He looks toward a brighter day and begins immediately to work toward it. His courage is contagious. His attitude prompts others to provide moral support and, in some cases, concrete ways of taking his next step forward.

One of his most powerful weapons against hopelessness is prayer. When his plans must be changed or, worse yet, when he is awaiting a decision on what his next step should be, he turns to his God for comfort. He believes fervently that God did not intend for him to be dejected and engulfed by this hopeless feeling. Of course, he knows too that God did not promise an easy, well-paved road to a fulfilling life. His prayers will not begin with "Dear God, take this feeling of hopelessness away from me" but rather "Dear God, help me to work through my feelings and to find specific actions that will restore my hope for the future."

Now comes the hard part. Look at your own life—your emotional problems, frustrations, anxieties, and any other aspect of importance to you. On a sheet of paper in your notebook, write down these various components of your life. As you write, if the feeling of hopelessness really has a viselike grip on you, your list will be quite lengthy. The list will probably include your handicap, the way you are feeling about that handicap right now, and your limitations.

Now, turn the tables on yourself. List as many positive components of your life as you can. Mull over each one. Think deeply about it. Savor it. Then ask yourself the crucial question: "With all of these positive components in mind, is my life really as hopeless as it seems? Or was I really dissatisfied over one particular phase of my life which blinded me from seeing all the others clearly?"

Next, look at the negative items on your list. Don't look at all the items at once, however. Concentrate on one at a time. Opposite each of them list one course of action that you can take that is short-term (two weeks or less) and one course of action that you can take that is long-term (up to six months). Do not make these plans overly complicated. Just decide upon one constructive action that you can take in each case. Now ask yourself, "If I can do these things about these particularly troublesome problem areas in my life, is my life really as hopeless as it seems?"

It's very important to the success of this exercise that you are as objective as possible. Should you look at one of these problem areas of your life and be unable to think of either a short- or long-term course of action, go on to the next one. Do not sit for an unduly long period of time brooding over any one item. For if you do, feelings of hopelessness that are already so near the surface of your emotions will only become that much stronger.

A reminder is appropriate at this point. If any one of the emotional problems explored in this chapter, or any other similar problem, does not respond to your efforts to deal with it, then it may be time to seek professional help. That is to say, we all have days when we feel angry, guilty, or hopeless. This is natural. But when these feelings persist despite all attempts we have made by ourselves or with family and friends to deal with them, it is time to look to the professional.

There is no disgrace to realizing that you need help and then searching for the type of help you need. There was a time, as many of us remember, when the stigma attached to consulting a psychologist, psychiatrist, minister, or other professional was very strong indeed. People believed that a person should be able to handle his own problems. It was a sign of weakness to admit that someone else's help was needed. Additionally, people's problems were thought to be their own private affair. Such matters were not to be discussed with anyone outside the immediate family. You were expected to accept your problems stoically, at least until you thought of some way to work them out. How blessed we are that such notions are all but extinct in modern society!

If people did not need help in coping with their problems, there would be no need for the dedicated men and women who enter psychology, psychiatry, or the ministry to choose these professions. As it is, many people have chosen to dedicate their lives to helping others in this way.

It is the people who turn their backs on their problems who are to be pitied, not those persons who admit to them and do something about them. As a handicapped person you are no different from anyone else. Though the specific nature of your emotional problems may differ from someone who is not handicapped, you have the same right and the same responsibility to yourself to seek this help, and to do so as soon as you believe it is necessary.

The professional person has several distinct advantages over family or friends or even over you yourself. First, he has received extensive training in problem-solving. He has been instructed in the most effective counseling techniques. This training, acquired over a period of years, will aid him in helping you to work through the problems with which you cannot cope on your own.

Second, he is largely objective. A member of your family or a close friend with whom you instinctively feel you want to share your problems cannot achieve that degree of objectivity easily.

Precisely because they love you and care about you, they see things from a biased point of view. The trained professional is interested in helping you work through your problems and will make every effort to show you that he *does* care about you. But he also will maintain a distance, a detachment that family or friends do not. It is that very feeling of detachment that allows him to take a hard look at the problems you present, and then make practical suggestions as to how you might manage them.

Bearing in mind the advantages of seeking professional help, however, you must not expect results overnight. Your emotional problems did not appear suddenly. Similarly, the logical working-out of these problems will in all likelihood not be a speedy process.

Additionally, there are no *right* or *wrong* solutions to your problems. The professional you consult cannot simply apply some mathematically proven formula to your set of circumstances and *presto!* have the right answer appear. But together, working with the professional, you can find ways of coping with these problems that will result in a healthier emotional makeup for you.

Finally, remember that your emotions are very complex. Your experiences play upon these emotions, and the result is the way you truly feel about yourself. Everyone has problems cropping up throughout his life. But know that it is within your power (sometimes with the help of others) to deal openly and honestly with these problems. You have what it takes. Be of good courage. Hold on just one minute longer! You *can* do it!

FIVE

The Spiritual Problems

The spiritual problems that confront handicapped people can be the most serious problems of all. But this is also true for persons who are not handicapped. As a guideline, let us once again turn to that famous piece, "Desiderata," which admonishes,

Therefore be at peace with God whatever you conceive him to be;

Any problem that prevents a person from being

at peace with his God is as damaging as ten floods and ten earthquakes combined.

The benefits of a God-centered life are many. When a person is at peace with his God, he is never alone. Always there is Someone to turn to, Someone to share things with, Someone who will understand. No problem—physical, mental, emotional, or otherwise—is too great or too small for God to handle. Remember, He can carry you through any problem or combination of problems. It will not be easy, but when you can communicate openly with Him, you are assured that an answer will be found.

With the many benefits of a God-centered life fixed firmly in your mind, it is not hard to see why any problems that stand in the way of such a life must be dealt with openly and promptly. There is no substitute for this, regardless of what material satisfaction you might think would lead to happiness. For God is the only constant, driving, uplifting Force in your life!

A personal experience brings this poignant truth to light. When I was a baby I had to have a very serious operation, without which I might have died within a matter of days or even hours. A nationally known neurosurgeon was to perform the surgery. Just before he entered the operating room, dressed in his surgical greens, he strode up to my father, his massive physical presence the epitome of strength, and said, "Reverend, where my work ends, yours and God's begins." Here was a great surgeon, perhaps the greatest man in his field at the time, who recognized the efficacy of prayer and the need for a strong, God-centered faith that would be unwavering in the face of any and all adversity. The surgeon's recognition of God's power in all our lives was unmistakable. He knew that even as he took the scalpel in his hand to make the incision, God was there. As he worked to insert the necessary tubes in this tiny infant, God was there. The operating room and the waiting room outside would be filled with a spirit of prayer and hopeful expectation. Only then was it possible for the surgeon to do his best work. Only then could he hope that the antici- pated result would become a reality, that the life of this tiny infant and countless others would be saved through the technique he had so recently perfected.

The obstacles that stand between you as an in- dividual and a full spiritual life are many. This is especially true if you are handicapped, because you could easily drown in your own sea of prob- lems. Let us look in detail at five spiritual prob- lems common to us as handicapped people in an effort to begin to resolve them.

The first spiritual problem is usually expressed as "Why has God done this to me?" Most people, handicapped or not, have asked this question when tragedy struck them or their loved ones per- sonally. How much more understandable it is for you as a handicapped person to raise this question. Your handicap is not temporary. It will not fade with the passage of time. You know that it is something that you will have to live with for the rest of your life.

As a teenager I went through a stage of mild depression when the reality of the permanence of my handicap struck with brutal force. It was difficult to discuss my feelings with anyone, for I felt almost wicked at the bitterness that was in my heart. "Why, God, why?" I must have asked that question a hundred times or more. One day when I could stand it no longer, I confided with the one person on earth I felt was most likely to understand—my own father, of course.

"Dad, what have I done to deserve this?" I asked him as we sat in his secluded den far away from the rest of the world. "Why has God done this to me?"

My father sat quietly for some time before he spoke. "I'm afraid you have the wrong attitude, my dear. The anger in your voice tells me that you feel somehow wronged or cheated by God." I winced. My father understood me so well! That is precisely the way I felt, but I had never been honest enough with myself to admit it before. He continued, "Your bitterness will get you no-where. So why not look at it another way? God made you different from other people. He took nearly all your physical sight away from you, but He allowed you to live when you could have died so easily on the operating table any number of times. What does that tell you?"

"I guess it tells me that He wanted me to live instead of to die," I said, not quite sure whether or not I understood his point.

"Exactly. God must have had a very special purpose in mind for you as He does for all His handicapped children. So why not spend your time praying for understanding as to what His purpose really is instead of sitting around feeling sorry for yourself? We all would have reason to do that if we wanted to, you know."

Then and there I decided to spend no more time feeling as if I had been dreadfully wronged by God. Instead, I would try to turn my thoughts from bitterness to anticipation of what God had in store for me!

Realizing that it is as understandable for you as it was for me to ask the question "Why has God done this to me?" however, does not mean that it can be answered accurately or that it is healthy for us to think this way. In fact, the very opposite is true. No earthly being can say for sure that he knows why you are handicapped. A doctor may be able to explain your handicap medically. But the deeper quesion, "Why?" is one that only God can answer.

Not only is asking such a question useless, because it cannot be answered while you are here on earth, but dwelling on such a question is in fact destructive. For it will lead you to manufacture all kinds of reasons in your mind as to why you are handicapped. While you are thinking these kinds of thoughts, you are taking time away from meaningful activities that could have a productive effect on your life.

It is a known fact that you are handicapped. It is also indisputable that God has a plan in mind for each of His children. Thus, if this is to be your lot in life, then accept it. Do not pause for even one moment to wonder why it is so!

A second spiritual problem, somewhat analogous to the first, is often phrased as "Am I being punished? Is the reason I am handicapped because I have committed some great sin against God?" Once again, attempts to analyze your handicap in such terms serve no useful purpose. It is a waste of time! We are all aware that every human being has faults, that everyone has said and done things that he wishes afterward he had not. But beyond that, to attempt to pick out our "worst sins" and then believe that it is to atone for those sins that God inflicted this handicap upon us would stunt our progress.

What is even more devastating about such thoughts is that if you think this way you are saying that your concept of God is a vengeful, get-even type God. "You have sinned against Me so I will pay you back!" I do not believe that this is the feeling that God in His infinite wisdom intends for His children to have about Him. Instead, is it not that God is a loving God? That He guides

His children in the path that He would have them take?

If you think of God as a loving God, you no longer worry about your sins being responsible for your handicap. All people have sinned at one time or another. People of strong faith will pray to God for forgiveness of those sins. They believe that He forgives all who truly repent. Thus, there is no room in their thinking for the idea that handicaps are doled out as punishments to "evil people."

A third spiritual problem is the feeling that "God has forgotten me." In this instance, the handicapped person feels that had God been "there" when he became handicapped, He would not have allowed it to happen. It is as though the person imagines that God takes periodic vacations. While He is on these vacations, He is not looking out for His children, but rather is off in a totally inaccessible place unable to remedy any plight that might befall a human being.

It would seem rather natural to adopt the God-has-forgotten-me theory if a person believes that when God is present in his life, only good and perfect things can come to him. Conversely, nothing that causes anguish or pain can come about when that same God is there. But think again. Back in biblical times people were faced with all types of problems—floods, famine, leprosy, and more. God was every bit as real to them as He can be to you today. Thus, the problems you face are mountains to climb with God's help, not things from which God-loving people can be exempted merely by attesting to their faith.

The Biblical passage "Wherever I am, God is" refutes the feeling that God could ever forget you. Similarly, God's protecting hand is ever-present. He will never forget you! God is not an on-again, off-again phenomenon. You can count on Him at all times! Always!

A fourth spiritual problem can best be described as "striking bargains with God." We have all had the tendency at one time or another to engage in this type of negotiation. Most commonly it is done in a prayer format. The prayer goes something like this: "Dear God, Please take this problem away from me. For if I no longer have this problem, it will be much easier for me to practice my faith. If it is taken away from me, I will go to church faithfully every Sunday, teach a Sunday school class, and even sing in the choir." It is as if we believe that we are sitting at the negotiating table with God. "You do this for me, and in return I will do that for You."

While I was in college I befriended an elderly lady who became like a grandmother to me. Having lost nearly all my grandparents as a young child, I craved the companionship of someone older and wiser during those somewhat turbulent years. This lady was as sweet as she was warm and friendly. Always interested in all my activities from school to church and everything in between, she could prompt me to discuss problems that I was unable to talk over with anyone else outside my own family. We spent many afternoons together having serious discussions or merely passing the hours having fun.

One day she became seriously ill with heart problems. The doctor advised a delicate surgical procedure, though he questioned whether she had the stamina to withstand it. "She may not survive, Gillian," my father warned me one day as we headed home from the hospital. "Don't be surprised if we get a call that she has passed away."

"But God won't let her *die*, Dad," I said with great conviction. "He knows how much her family loves her, how much I love her and need her!"

But suddenly I was not so sure. That night I resolved that I would ask God to spare her life. In return, I would offer to do some extra work at our church, take on added responsibilities at home, and even help around the house more willingly than I had up to now. Surely, in exchange for all that, God won't let her die! I thought as I prayed more intently than ever before.

But God did "let" her die. In His infinite wisdom He determined that it was time for her to take the place He had prepared for her. Though in my mind I knew that she would not have wanted to go on living hooked up to a wide range of machines, unable to enjoy the home she loved, my heart was aching. And all the while I wondered, didn't I offer God enough in exchange for what I asked of Him? For many months thereafter I was unwilling to admit that regardless of your good intentions, you cannot strike a bargain with God!

Once again, handicapped persons find themselves more susceptible to this kind of bargaining than nonhandicapped people. The handicaps we face are so devastating that we believe they are more than we can bear—more than we should have to bear. The best way we know to try to rid ourselves of our handicaps is to strike up a bargain with God.

However, we must remember that our handicaps are within the scope of God's plan for us. He gave us the strength to see us through. Therefore, to think that we could bargain away a part of what God had in mind for us is out of the question.

God knows the strengths and weaknesses of each of His children. It is therefore reassuring to know that He will not fill the plate of any one of us with more than He believes we are capable of handling. What is more, if the task seems too great, we are always at liberty to pray to Him for additional strength and forbearance. And He will answer!

The fifth spiritual problem is "What is God's purpose for me?" This is a difficult question to ponder until you have learned to cope with the daily routine that your particular handicap dictates. For a time it is nearly impossible to see beyond your handicap itself. However, eventually, nearly everyone progresses beyond the stage of preoccupation with daily tasks and begins to be concerned with the higher question of establishing a purpose for his life.

Even as a small child I wanted a sense of purpose in my daily activities, although I was unable to participate in specific phases of school life. A very wise teacher was preparing my class for a special events competition in a variety of physical exercises. One of the competitions involved jumping rope. Each student was to take his turn and continue jumping until he missed. The student who jumped the longest would become the champion. I was not able to participate, because I had neither the sight nor the coordination to jump rope. What is more, there was a strong possibility that if I tried to do it, I could hurt myself badly. It broke my heart that I could not jump rope too.

But God had another purpose for me. As time neared for my classmates to start their practice sessions, my teacher approached me and asked if I would be willing to turn one end of the jump rope while she turned the other. Together, my teacher and I would make it possible for the other children to compete. Needless to say, God through this very perceptive teacher turned a negative experience into a positive one and prevented me from wallowing in self-pity. The warmth and pride on my face the day of the competition was nothing short of complete. For I had won a victory all my own—being included as a part of my peer group on a level that was both attainable and useful. A gift God had given me, strength in my arms, could be put to use to help my classmates.

Of course, as has been pointed out earlier, only God Himself could authoritatively answer the question "What is God's purpose for me?" But unlike asking yourself why your handicap occurred or what you have done wrong to deserve it, there is some value to be derived from pondering the question.

For example, in my case, I believe that the main reason God made me legally blind is so that I can share my feelings, aspirations, and frustrations with other handicapped people, their families, friends, teachers, counselors, and potential employers. Perhaps if I had been fully sighted, I would not have put such energy into public speaking and writing. If I can, through any type of communication, ease the burden on someone else's shoulders or assure them that they are not alone, then a major purpose of my life will have been fulfilled. This and any other purpose that God should have for me can be carried out in spite of or perhaps even because of my handicap.

God gives each of us not only special strengths but special gifts as well. It is essential that you discover what these gifts are in your case and then use them in a way that will bring satisfaction of the highest kind into your life. The result will be a feeling of happiness that far exceeds anything you have ever experienced before.

God will guide us through all our spiritual problems. If we but put our trust in Him, He will make His way clear to us. We must remember, however, that this may not come about instantly. As we search for solutions to our spiritual problems, it is the end result that we pursue. But He may see the great value for us in the search process itself. Periods of darkness and uncertainty, for example, may be used to bolster a weakened faith. For during such times we instinctively turn to a higher power when we see the futility of our continuing to plod along without God's help. As God seeks to see us develop spiritually, He may offer challenges in forms that are unusual, difficult, or even remote.

Think back to the times of relative tranquillity in your life. Are these the times when you have felt surges of spiritual growth? Did you feel a sense of spiritual achievement? Probably not. While you may have been grateful for the positive events that were taking place in your life and you may have paused in genuine thanksgiving to God, it is likely that the fibers of your spiritual faith were not tested.

But think again—this time about the trials in your life. Perhaps it was uncertainty about a medical outcome or problems concerning employment or finances. As you made it through these times with God's help, did you not feel a deeper closeness with Him? Perhaps you thought about stories you read as a child in the Bible about people who triumphed over all types of adversity. While when you were a child those readings may have seemed unreal to you, didn't they take on a new meaning?

It is natural for you to want peace and happy times to predominate in your life. But it is during those times that you can also prepare yourself for the uncertain or unpleasant experiences that will undoubtedly arise. This does not mean being a prophet of doom who always anticipates the worst possible outcome even when things are progressing well. It does not mean looking at the negative side of every issue. Rather, it means using the somewhat more tranquil times in your life to converse with God and to build up the resources that will help you meet the crises of tomorrow. Then when the need arises, your mind and soul will be in tune with God. You will have an anchor to hold on to during your own traumatic experiences. No matter what the situation may be, you can call upon God as you would upon a trusted and loyal friend. And your call for help will always be answered! God will respond, though perhaps not in the way that you would expect. But he will respond in His way—and His way is truly the right way!

God is there. He is a resource for each and

every one of us to tap. He will not let you down. In times of spiritual need you can always call upon Him! He loves all His children fully and completely. You are His child. His love is waiting for *you*!

SIX

The Social
Problems

In the preceding chapters we have examined our major problems as handicapped individuals. Now we will broaden our perspective and consider the problems we face as we attempt to take our place in society.

Of course, not all of us will experience the same social problems any more than we experience the same physical, mental, emotional, or spiritual problems. Nor will the social problems we *do* experience take on the same degree of significance for all of us. Bearing these differences in mind, however, there remain some very critical social needs of the handicapped that must be addressed. These needs will not be met easily. We as handicapped people must do our part to identify and communicate our social needs to the community at large. With our dedication and their help we will succeed!

Let us now consider four social problems believed by many handicapped people to be major stumbling blocks that stand between them and a full life. The first is the need to be needed. We cry out, "If I am not of some use, then why am I here on this earth?" We need to believe that our lives have a special purpose—a role that only we can fulfill.

Frequently, when people deal with the handicapped they are so concerned about helping us that they do not realize that as individuals, we too need to be of service to others. True, it is sometimes more difficult to find an area in which a handicapped person can serve effectively, but it is essential that such areas be found.

I recall my feeling of utter uselessness as a child when the time came to trim our family Christmas tree each year. This is one of the few times I felt I did not have my dad's understanding. Dad would bring the tree in from outdoors, and then he and my sister would work on finding the best side of it to face the front. He would get down on his knees, grab the trunk, and turn it while she stood and looked from a distance.

There was nothing for me to do. "You can't see. You wouldn't know when it was right anyway," they would admonish me when I would offer my opinion.

Later, when it came time to string the colored lights on the tree, my services were again refused. "You can't see what branches to string them on so they would be balanced," my sister would say with hardly a thought of guiding my hand so I could hang at least one string of lights. Then she and Dad would continue to work on it. He would place lights on the upper boughs, and in later years, when she grew taller, she took over that task, too.

In contrast, I can remember the joyous feeling of being needed for a school project. It involved putting together a small literary magazine of stories and poems written by us seventh graders. No one was told in advance whether or not his story or poem had been chosen for publication. When the day came, I found that a short story of mine had been selected. "We really needed that story," my teacher told me. "All the other students submitted short poems and I'm sure the parents will also enjoy reading something that has a plot to it." My joy at meeting this need can best be described by the fact that with my face beaming, I literally ran the six blocks home to tell my parents. The faster I ran, the harder it became to keep my balance. But I was so excited that I scarcely noticed.

As I have grown older I have never lost that need to feel needed. Instead, it has intensified. When someone I know is ill, I try to help him in some small way. If a person has a problem, I hope to be the one with whom he would feel comfortable discussing it. If there is a job to be done for which I believe I am qualified and where I may be able to make a contribution, I want nothing more than to be selected for that job.

Some people might think that I carry this need almost to an extreme. Perhaps they are right. I suspect that the intensity of my desire to be useful dates back to the early years of my childhood when nearly everything was done *for* me. All those years, I was denied accepting even a small share of my responsibilities for fear that I would break or damage something, or even hurt myself. I was willing to take that risk, but my family and friends were not. Denying me the opportunity to do my part did more damage than breaking an object or hurting myself would have ever done. They believed they were doing me a favor, but there is little doubt in my mind that one of the worst things that someone can do to a handicapped person, albeit unintentionally, is to rob him or her of the opportunity to feel needed and to be useful.

Americans today believe that much of what is wrong with our country is that so many people are preoccupied with what they can get out of life rather than what they can put into it. In contrast, most handicapped persons are searching for ways to give of themselves because they have had to accept help from so many different sources for so long just to survive.

As a handicapped person, you must be given the opportunity to prove that you too can be of service. You may have to make adjustments, for the area in which you may wish to serve may not always be the area in which you are capable of serving. For example, a handicapped friend of mine had been hospitalized and was so impressed with the service rendered by the people who brought the snack cart in the evenings, he vowed he would volunteer for that role when he recovered from his surgery.

The volunteer coordinator appreciated his positive attitude and understood his need to be of service. However, because of his limited mobility, she offered him an assignment at the receptionist desk instead, where he was just as useful.

Like my friend, you must be flexible as you offer to be of service. If you are, opportunities will come more readily to you.

A second major social problem is that of satisfying our need to compete. By competition I am speaking of a healthy rivalry between two or more persons in a specific endeavor. For the nonhandicapped person competition is a means by which he can evaluate his own skills and talents by measuring them against his opponents. For the handicapped person competition fulfills this same need.

Once again, however, the handicapped person finds himself at a decided disadvantage. He is caught between seeking adjustments to the traditional rules as a compensation for his handicap or being silent about his disadvantage and struggling along as best he can.

One of the favorite activities of our sixth-grade math class was a competition. The teacher had a set of flash cards, each containing a short mathematical problem. One student would begin by standing next to the desk behind him and seeing whether he could solve the problem faster than the student seated, against whom he was competing. If he succeeded, he would move on to the next desk. He was able to continue until someone seated responded quicker than he did. He would then have to take the seat of that particular student. The challenge was to get as far away from your original seat as possible.

When the teacher stood at the front of the room, I could not see the numbers on her flash cards. Thus, I had to choose between failing in the competition because I was unable to see or speaking up so that she would come closer by for me to see the numbers accurately. It was a tough decision to make, because I did not want to draw undue attention to myself. But I finally decided that it was far worse to appear as though I did not know the answer to the problem than it was to ask her to stand where I could see the cards.

The key to meeting this need to compete most effectively is to find an endeavor where your particular disability is of least importance. That is, the area of competition you choose should favor your talents and minimize your disabilities. This is really no different from the approach taken by a nonhandicapped person except that it may take longer to select your area of competitive activity. Take your time in making your selection. Look at it from all angles. Ask any questions to clarify your understanding. In other words, make an intelligent decision!

Once you have selected an area of competition, you may still be at a disadvantage compared to the other participants because of your handicap. If this is true, you have two basic options. One is that you can simply ignore your disadvantage and try that much harder to compete successfully operating under all the traditional rules. The other option is that you can seek out the person in charge of the competition, explain your situation accurately and concisely, and see just how willing that individual is to make adjustments.

If you choose the latter course of action, as I did in the math competition, it is much better if you have in mind the adjustments that you would like to see made *before* you approach the person in charge. Be specific in telling him exactly what you want him to do. Be realistic in your expectations. Be willing to compromise. In this way, that individual will know that you have given the matter much thought and are not simply making ridiculous demands. Also, he will see that the competition must be very meaningful to you if you have taken the time and effort to think through necessary modifications.

Regardless of which option you choose, do not expect much sympathy or understanding from your fellow competitors. This does not mean that they do not care about you as a person or that they are insensitive to your handicap. But for the period of time that the competition lasts, they are your opponents. They are out to win! This is the best reason for advance planning and for discussion to take place only between you and the person in charge.

Learn from your experience. Do not be afraid to come to the decision that the initial area of competition you chose is not really the right one for you. Nonhandicapped persons alter their course in midstream when that is necessary. Why should you be any different?

Know in advance how to win and lose graciously. This is important for everyone, but especially for you. For people will be watching you closely to see if you use your handicap as an excuse for poor performance. Know that when you do not win, it does not mean that you have failed. What it means is that you need more practice, different modifications, or a different area of competition altogether.

Above all, do not give up. This is the time for an extra portion of courage mixed with a large helping of determination. Whereas an activity may come very easily to someone else, you may have to work twice as hard to accomplish the same skill because of your handicap. But if you enjoy it, if you find it satisfying, you will not mind the work. For you will see it as an opportunity to prove something to those people who may have doubts as to your ability or determination. You will perceive it as an opportunity to prove something to yourself. You will show yourself that you do have what it takes to compete in the real world! You are not afraid! You have attributes like everyone else and you welcome the opportunity to use those attributes in a healthy, competitive framework.

A third social problem is the need for handicapped persons to join a group and to be accepted as a contributing member of that group. There are a number of reasons why such group affiliation is important to us. To begin with, many things can be accomplished collectively that cannot be done individually. "There is strength in numbers" is an old saying but a true one.

In my community a number of individuals spoke frequently about the need to have specific parking spaces designated for handicapped persons. They felt that it would be much easier for people with a wide variety of disabilities to have access to stores and other business places if they would be assured of a parking space close by. Although much discussion took place on the subject, nothing specific was actually accomplished until one day several people decided to band together to work on the project. They formed a group and approached members of our city council and city administrators with the problem. Though the results were by no means immediate, our city officials were forced to take notice of this need because a number of people spoke to them about it. They were all part of a group that had done its homework, presented its figures, and articulately expressed its need. As a result, we now have handicapped parking spaces along our city streets. What is more, a number of local merchants, taking the city's lead, believed that they could increase their business if they too would provide such spaces. Thus, a specific need perceived by a number of individual people grew into a citywide project when they formed a group to accomplish their purpose. This same group remained together and has tackled a number of other problems in a similar fashion.

But the need to be part of a group goes far deeper than the desire to achieve specific goals. This is particularly important for a handicapped person, since at times he may feel isolated by his handicap. Group affiliation attests to the fact that "you are not alone. There are other people with your problems or interests."

A young mother whose son was confined to a wheelchair observed that even when he was surrounded by a large group of children, her son often looked dejected and lonely. She surmised—correctly, I believe—that many of the things the youngsters were talking about or doing did not relate to her son's activities. Since he could not identify with the other children's conversation, he felt left out. Sometime later, when she and her son were alone, she casually suggested that he might wish to make friends with other children who also had a handicap. She told him that he would be able to help them in some ways, and they would be able to help him in others. There would be many things they could find to do together. Her son chose to make friends with both groups of youngsters. He did not confine his friends to handicapped children only but did find that he enjoyed the company of handicapped as well as nonhandicapped children.

Therefore, to avoid this feeling of being left out of group discussions, do as the young boy did. Select your group carefully as you seek to fulfill your need for group affiliation. But before you can begin your selection process, you will need to understand what it is that you hope to gain from the group interaction that you seek. Are you looking for a social group? Do you want a group that will teach you a new skill or help you to perfect a skill that you already possess? Are you interested in a specific cause that would be easier to champion if you were part of a group? After you have answered these questions, you will be in a much better position to explore the groups available in your area.

Find out the name of a person who is already a member of any group you are seriously considering joining. Give that person a call and let him know that you are interested in his group. People enjoy talking about groups they belong to, so you should have little trouble in getting additional facts and having your questions answered.

If you are interested, ask if you may attend a regular meeting or other activity of the particular group. Do not expect too much the first time you attend, or you may be setting yourself up for a needless disappointment. When you go to a meeting or activity, keep an open mind about your possible future involvement. Do not allow an overly zealous member to pressure you into joining "on the spot." Join only if you agree with the group's objectives, if you feel at ease with its members, and if you are ready to make a commitment.

A word of caution: Guard against being a compulsive joiner. Instead, be selective so that you will be able to gain as well as give to the group you choose.

When I was in high school, I became interested in the speech and forensics group. After a few days I had ambitious ideas about competing in a large interscholastic tournament. While my enthusiasm was appreciated and may have inspired some of the more seasoned members who were becoming complacent, it took the speech coach some time to bring me down to earth. She explained in detail the rules governing such competition, the seniority system of our own school's program, and the requirements for the speech itself. The more I listened, the more discouraged I became. It seemed that it would be forever before I would be able to use my speaking skills.

In reality, it was only about two weeks before I began competing in interscholastic tournaments, but it seemed an eternity to me. I worked very hard on my speech, but it didn't seem to be progressing fast enough. Had I researched the team's requirements and procedures more carefully beforehand, I would have known that the process of perfecting a speech and entering a competition was detailed and time-consuming. And I would have saved myself the disappointment at what I thought was my own slow progress.

Even after you have decided that you want to join a particular group, there will be disappointments. For rarely, if ever, do the wishes of the group correspond with yours one hundred percent of the time. These disappointments should not make you overly discouraged, however. Wait for a time until the particular project you do not enthusiastically support is completed. Lend what support you can, but do not feel that you must participate in everything with an equal amount of zeal and conviction. Be prepared for a period of learning as you begin to see the group's activities from the inside as a member instead of from the outside as an interested observer. The more you learn, the more you will be able to contribute when the time comes.

Do not undertake too large a task as you begin your involvement in any group. For if you do, you may become overwhelmed and discouraged. You may begin to question your involvement in the group simply because you have "gotten in over your head" in the beginning.

By following these steps, you will be a better member of any group you join. You will contribute all that you can and stand ready to assume greater responsibilities as time passes. Yours will be the type of membership that any group will welcome. Your ideas will add something unique to the group's efforts. Both you and the organization will be better off as a result!

A fourth social problem is the need for guidance in our quest to feel closer to a higher Power. For most of us it is necessary to receive this guidance because we cannot achieve such a closeness alone. Ministers, teachers, close friends, and even our parents could be of great help to us as we struggle to develop a deeper relationship with God, but very often even they feel inadequate to approach the subject of the handicapped person and his God.

We have already determined that particularly at times of great stress or hardship, we will need to have faith in Someone who possesses infinite strength, wisdom, and love for us—faith in our God.

When I was a child in the hospital, I felt very much alone. My father, who had been my strength and support ever since I could remember, told me that he would not be allowed to accompany me to the operating room. This had been true before, of course, but then I had been too young to understand. This time the reality of my separation from him when I felt I needed him the most was almost more than I could bear. I was trying very hard to be his "good soldier," as he called me, but I just wasn't having much luck.

A short time before the cart was to take me to surgery, Dad, in his understanding way, sat down beside my bed and began to talk softly. "You'd like me to go with you to surgery, wouldn't you?"

"Oh, yes, Daddy. Won't you please?" I was almost begging by this time.

"Well, I've told you that I am not allowed in the operating room with all the doctors and nurses who will be there trying to make you better. But how would it be if Someone were to go with you in my place?"

"Who, Daddy?" By this time I was so curious

about whom he had in mind that I had almost forgotten all about being afraid.

"God will go with you in my place. He loves you so much, even more than I do. So you couldn't have anyone better."

"Will He be smiling at me like you do?" I wanted to know.

"God smiles down on all His children when they admit that they need Him," Dad explained.

From that moment on I felt less frightened. I really believed that everything was going to be all right. Not only because Dad said that it would be but because there *would* be Someone with me while the surgery was taking place.

Later, when I was awake and back in my room, Dad asked me if I remembered anything from the operation. "Just feeling safe," I said. And that was very true, for to this day the entire experience of that particular hospital stay revolves around that very special moment.

As I grow older, I remember that day each time I have found myself in a stress-filled situation. I am grateful for the guidance I received that helped me to develop that closeness with God. You too can receive the same type of guidance from a minister, a teacher, a close friend, or your parents if you just help them to be at ease with your handicap and let them know how vital their guidance can be to you.

To begin with, reassure the person you have chosen to confide in that simply because you are handicapped does not mean that he should treat you in any special way. You are just like any other person who is seeking this same closeness to God. Tell him that the only difference between you and a nonhandicapped person in this case is that you may feel a more intense or more frequent need because of the varied problems your handicap creates.

Be totally honest with the person you have chosen to help you. Do not be afraid to admit to him that your faith is not as strong as you would like it to be. No one was ever criticized for admitting a weakness, particularly if he was willing to do something about it.

You must also be willing to ask God to strengthen your faith and the resolve of the person who is trying to help you. This may be difficult at first because you are not accustomed to admitting your weaknesses—even to God. Seeking God's strength will help both you and your spiritual counselor. Remember, God knows everything about you as a person. He will not ridicule you or cause you embarrassment as you turn to Him for direction.

Reassure your counselor that although your need is great, you do not expect results overnight. Tell him that you know you will stumble and fall as you walk through this time of spiritual growth but that with God and your counselor by your side, you will ultimately succeed in developing a close relationship with God and a powerful faith.

One of the greatest women I know has undergone numerous surgeries for a variety of cancer-related health problems. One day I asked her if she ever felt depressed or fearful about what course the cancer would take. "Never," she said with such deep conviction that I knew she could be speaking only the truth.

"Why not?" I asked, sincerely wondering why she would be any different from other cancer victims I had known, who were somewhat downcast and pessimistic at times.

"Because," she said simply, "I know that underneath me at all times are God's everlasting arms. He will never pull His arms out from under me. He will always be there no matter what happens."

Faith like my friend's need not be a dream or an unrealistic goal for you. It is available right now. Today. Reach for it. Pray about it. With your spiritual counselor's help, ask God to guide you as you strive to attain it. You will possess that total faith! Once you have it, it will burn like an eternal flame inside you for the rest of your life. You will want to share it with others. The more you share it, the stronger it will grow. You are God's creation. You have the power to seek and enrich your faith. Don't put it off! Begin now!

SEVEN

The Problem of the Public's Reactions

In the preceding chapter we reviewed our social problems as handicapped people striving to make a place for ourselves in America today. Now we are ready to go a step further and consider the ultimate problem of the public's reactions to us and our ability to improve the relationship between us and the rest of the world.

The most famous saying of the poet John Donne, "No man is an island, entire of itself," best illustrates our problem. Indeed, every handicapped person interacts with other people many times in a given day. What makes us different from nonhandicapped people is that we are very likely to get undesirable reactions from them simply because any handicap makes them uncomfortable.

You may say, "I don't care what people think about me. I have to live my life my way, regardless." But is that *really* true? Think about it. Almost everyone wants people to respond to them in a positive way. In this respect, once again we are no different from anyone else.

Even if other people's opinions have never been particularly important to you, look at it this way. You need to understand those opinions and reactions so that you will be able to deal with them. Remember, it is *your* responsibility to achieve this understanding insofar as possible, because you have the most to gain—or lose!

Additionally, there will always be those people who are confused as to how they should behave or respond to a handicapped person. You must be able to take the lead in such situations! If you are kind and understanding where they are concerned, most people will make every effort to show a similar attitude toward you.

A good example of this occurred one day when I was invited to a buffet dinner by members of a church committee. After the waitress had taken our order for the buffet, a period of awkward silence followed. Finally I said, "Shall we go for our salad?" Two of the committee members exchanged puzzled glances but said nothing. I rose and slowly walked to the salad table. They followed closely. I picked up a plate and began selecting from the many salads available.

"I can't believe it!" mumbled one member to another. "She did that all by herself!" By this time it was becoming increasingly difficult for me to remain quiet. When we returned to the table, one man said to me, "We worried about how much help you might need and how to offer our assistance without embarrassing you."

"Thank you so much," I said sincerely. "Actually, I can manage quite well most of the time. But when I need a little help, I'll ask for it and perhaps one of you could lend a hand." Everyone was very relieved. Their sighs were almost audible. I was happy that I could put them at ease, and it made the remainder of the meal much more enjoyable for everyone. When I did need some assistance cutting a piece of meat from the buffet platter, I had more than the required number of willing helpers.

Ultimately, your success in life will be determined to a large extent by the quality of the relationships you form with other people. Do your part to develop these relationships to the fullest!

There are, of course, numerous reactions that members of the general public will have toward you as a handicapped person. Some of the more common reactions will be treated individually in this chapter. By attempting to understand these reactions, you will also be in a better position to deal with the less common responses you may receive.

As a start toward gaining this understanding, put yourself in a nonhandicapped person's shoes. Most of the people he knows are not handicapped. His frame of reference may include only one or two persons who are handicapped. Or perhaps no one at all. Thus, his lack of experience may have a great deal to do with his reactions toward you.

Also, remember that many people react first with their emotions. They will allow their prejudices to have free reign until you give them reason to do otherwise. Most likely, they will not give you the benefit of the doubt in the beginning. This explains the statement that we as handicapped people often make: "If people thought about it, they wouldn't feel this way." That's just it, they don't think—not at first, anyway. They simply react. Finally, remember that the reactions that we as handicapped people dislike so intensely are usually not borne out of malice against us as individuals. Instead, they are often borne out of insecurity, ignorance, or fear.

The reactions discussed here may seem improbable or even archaic as you read and think about them. "Surely no one still feels that way," you may say. But the unvarnished truth is that many people are still back in the Stone Age when it comes to their attitudes about handicapped people. While medical advances in treating handicaps have been numerous in recent years, the reactions of other people have not kept pace. In fact, they lag far behind. Though on an intellectual level people may espouse such terms as "equality" and "fairness" in relation to the handicapped, in many cases they give lip service only. They do not translate these ideals into everyday practice. It is the real world we are dealing with, not the way we would like things to be!

The first reaction, and perhaps the most antiquated one of all, is that handicapped people are what is often referred to as "God's little mistakes." People holding this view believe that even God is entitled to err once in a while as He creates human beings.

I wish that these people had been exposed to a favorite Sunday school teacher of mine who once built an entire lesson around the theme "God created us all." When one of the youngsters asked, "Even Gillian, who can hardly see? Why would He do that?" the teacher responded, "Yes, He created people like Gillian and took much of her sight away. But He arranged to make up for it in other ways. That's the way it is with all His children. He may give them less of one thing, but He more than makes up for it."

By the time she had finished, not only the youngster who had first posed the question, but all of the children, knew that God never makes mistakes. He knows exactly what He is doing as

He carefully places each one of us here on this earth with special plans in mind for what we will do while we are here.

People who hold the God's-little-mistakes view believe that handicapped people are a type of subhuman species. It follows that if handicapped people are less than full human beings, then they are not really worthy of serious consideration. Their needs are not important, and their views mean nothing at all.

However, some of us believe that any person who lacks a healthy perception of the handicapped should become a "project" for us to undertake. Our instinct is to plunge in and do what we can to reason with these people so that they will get an accurate picture of us. Yet this is one time when we must suppress our instincts. Some people have "just made up their minds." Letting go of these people will be difficult, but is essential.

A second reaction can best be termed as the don't-touch-me syndrome. The people who respond to us in this way have in many cases an unhealthy fear that "it will rub off," as if being handicapped were a type of communicable disease.

Perhaps the only positive thing to be said about this is that at least these people acknowledge that the handicapped person is a human being too. Thus, they have made limited progress beyond the God's-little-mistakes concept.

A good illustration of this is the mother who, coming upon her son playing in the schoolyard after school, said to him, "Come along and play over here, dear. You'll not be quite as close to that boy over there!" as she made a sweeping gesture in the direction of a wheelchair-bound youngster who was playing marbles with another friend.

"What's wrong with him?" her son asked, obviously at this point unaffected by his mother's bias.

Her response? "Don't ask questions, dear. Just do as mother says." She was, of course, unwilling to offer any explanation to her son of her own prejudice. What is most tragic of all in this case is that explanation or none, the mother's feelings may at some point "rub off" on her son!

With people who react in this way the only hope is that someday they will be forced by circumstances into contact with a handicapped person. And if that handicapped person is pleasant to them, confident in himself, and very tolerant through his positive attitude, he will be able to chip away at their bias.

A third reaction of the public, and one that is extremely common, is pity. "Oh, the poor dear!" is this person's first thought when he meets someone who is handicapped. People who feel this way may talk to you about "the cross you have to bear" or "the curse that has befallen you." They truly believe that you are a pathetic soul, doomed to live out the remainder of your years in some type of half life.

One of the members of the church I attended as a youngster fit almost perfectly into this category. Every time she saw me I knew before she uttered a word that she believed I was indeed a pathetic soul. "How do you cope from day to day knowing that the poor child will always be abnormal?" she asked my father one day.

"I suppose we cope because we don't think in such terms," my father answered her. "We just take everything one day at a time, do all that we can for Gillian, and leave the rest in God's hands."

Unfortunately the woman must not have heard my father, because for as long as I knew her, she seemed amazed that I wanted to continue to live even though I would always be "in such a pitiful state of affairs."

These people ignore the fact that you may possess a fighting spirit, courage, ingenuity, or motivation. To them you are someone who would be better off dead than "sentenced to continue living."

The main problem with such people is that they are rarely capable of any constructive action. Once they have found an outlet for their emotion in the form of pity for you, they dismiss you as "a lost cause" and move on. They feel they have done their part. Therefore, it is unlikely that any of them would ever stop to think how they might help you or enhance the quality of your life.

With this segment of the population, however, you must take every opportunity you can to demonstrate that you do not pity yourself nor do you need their pity. Pity serves no purpose. It will neither help you nor provide any genuine satisfaction for them.

On a bus tour of an animal preserve I was sitting next to a woman with whom I had a passing acquaintance. Though she was aware of my visual handicap, we had never discussed it. "It's such a shame that you can't see the pretty birds very clearly," she said in that readily recognizable pitying tone of voice. "They are really beautiful. You're missing a lot!"

In as kind a tone as I could muster, and with every effort that my anger should not gain control, I replied, "Perhaps, but I can hear their sweet songs very well. Aren't their voices beautiful?" In this way I was able to show her that I was not dwelling on what I could *not* enjoy but instead was focusing my attention on what I *could* appreciate.

A fourth reaction of many people is to feel that if a person is handicapped in one area, then he is likely handicapped in other ways as well. These people have a difficult time differentiating between the kinds and the degrees of various handicaps. A friend of mine who is totally blind was once eating out with some of her sighted friends.

The waitress observed my friend's guide dog lying quietly at her feet and so was aware that she was blind. As the waitress was going around the table taking orders, she noted the selection of the man seated next to my friend and then said, "And what would *she* like to eat?"

The young man, a champion of the handicapped, said sharply, "I don't know. Why don't you ask her? She'll tell you." The waitress, red-faced and embarrassed, became keenly aware of what she had done. She had assumed that simply because my friend was blind that she could not read the menu. The waitress never thought that my friend would have asked someone in advance about what was on the menu, made her selection, and been ready to give her order.

In this case the young man's motivation was clear. In as strong a way as he could think of, he was trying to point up the waitress's mistake to her. Just because a customer was blind did not mean that she could not give her order.

However, it should also be pointed out that the young man used the wrong approach. Embarrassing the waitress may have taught her a lesson, but it did not win a friend for handicapped people. In fact, the waitress may shy away from a handicapped person in the future because she would not want to run the risk of making a similar mistake again.

How much better it would have been if the young man had answered the question by turning to my friend and asking, "What would you like to eat?" In this way the waitress could witness her mistake and hear for herself that my friend could communicate without any problem. There was no need to cause embarrassment.

People who lump "the handicapped" into a single category like so many pieces of candy in a box must learn that there are as many different types of handicaps as there are people who have them. Again, these people must be shown that, for example, being blind does not make a person automatically deaf and lame also. This is a matter of educating the public.

In many cases it may take a specific experience, such as that of the waitress in the restaurant, before people will detect an error in their thinking. Once they have had such an experience, it is not easily forgotten. The embarrassment they suffered will remind them that each person's handicap must be considered singly. Armed with this knowledge, they are eager indeed to share it with other people. So it is very likely that the multiplier effect will be started and other people will be the beneficiaries of their experience.

A fifth reaction to handicapped people is that all of them belong in residential institutions, away from "normal" people. Persons who feel this way have recognized that handicapped people do exist, but believe there should be special places for them. The handicapped should not be permitted to mix with society as a whole. It is as if they accept the fact that there are handicapped people in the world, but do not want to be reminded of it. "Out of sight, out of mind," is their view.

I can remember a schoolmate's mother talking with my parents about "a wonderful special school for blind children like Gillian, where she would be with her own kind." As she explained about the school, which was no doubt a fine facility, it was as if she were more concerned about having me placed in a school outside our city than she was about the quality of the school. When my father suggested that he believed a regular school to be the best thing for his daughter as long as she was making good grades and able to keep pace with only minor adjustments, the woman said, "Yes, but think what you are exposing the other children to. Don't you care what happens to them?"

"And just what *are* we exposing the other children to?" my father wanted to know.

"Why, they have to see a different type of child with a handicap every day!" she said as though that were the worst thing a child could behold. "They don't understand what they are seeing. They just know it makes them uncomfortable to be around her!"

"Oh, I doubt that they'll be uncomfortable very long," my father countered. "Gillian puts everybody at ease pretty quickly. She'll let them know that she doesn't regard her handicap as anything more threatening than another child would regard the braces he wears on his teeth!"

I believe these people know, deep down in their souls, that their attitude is prejudicial and unjust. To soothe their conscience, however, they rationalize, "Handicapped people are really better off with their own kind because they won't feel so inferior to us that way," or they might say, "Handicapped people are better off in an institution where they can be protected from the hazards of society." They bury their own bias securely underneath a façade of having the handicapped person's best interest at heart.

This viewpoint is nurtured by the fact that there are specific cases in which people with handicaps *are* better served by being institutionalized, such as when they have no family and require constant care. What is more, these handicapped people are often the ones who receive the publicity, and that fact only enhances this particular belief.

When you come into contact with these people, your very presence will shake their belief to its roots. You may see them at a meeting or on the street. You are not in an institution. You are "out among them" and functioning. Thus, here again, your example is the most powerful weapon you have. If "seeing is believing" to these people, then indeed they will have seen. It will remain for them only to believe.

A sixth public reaction to the handicapped is that feeling of uneasiness at being around us.

They are uncertain how they should behave. For example, is it all right to say something to you about your handicap? Is it acceptable to ask "How are you?" or is that taboo?

A family friend once told my father, "I feel funny when I'm around Gillian. She seems to be happy and jolly. But I figure that she is just bluffing because I can't understand how someone who is legally blind could really be that happy. I don't know whether to try to get close to her by probing for her real feelings or to just accept her as she is and be happy right along with her." By her tone of voice she conveyed the feeling that I had no right to be happy.

"You may as well be happy," my father said to her a trifle tartly, "because whether you believe it or not, she really is! I call her 'my sunshine girl!'"

Though the woman's comment may have aggravated my father at the time, it points up the fact that many people expect us to be sad and bitter. Perhaps they would be more comfortable dealing with that type of attitude. But in most cases we are not.

With these people there is a good chance that our positive attitude will have more than its usual impact. For they are aware not only that the handicapped are a part of society just as other human beings are, but they are also aware that interaction between "them" and "us" is a natural occurrence. Their problem comes with not knowing how to respond.

As always, it is easier for nonhandicapped people to interact with us when we are basically well adjusted and happy at being ourselves. The more they see us as congenial people, the better they will adjust to us.

Again, these people will share their experiences with others. So, in effect, our positive attitude and healthy interactions with them will make it easier for other handicapped people they may meet in the future.

A seventh reaction to the handicapped is the attitude of "peaceful coexistence." People who share this view know that handicapped people exist and that they have a right to exist. But they feel that this existence should take place "over there," "away from me, away from my family." These people do not really care whether or not the handicapped are institutionalized, whether or not they have jobs, just as long as they do not have to be involved with the handicapped in any way.

I was required to take a biology course as a high school sophomore. A difficult task at best because of the many lab experiments that were required, this class was pure torture for me. I was unable to measure accurately, dissect with precision, and tabulate our results on attractively drawn, sophisticated graphs. These limitations made it very difficult to work with my capable lab partner.

"You just can't do anything right," he fumed at

me one day. At last I could stand it no longer. I went up to the instructor quietly and explained the problem at the conclusion of that day's lab.

"He just wants you to be like the other kids," the teacher said with almost a complete lack of understanding. "He doesn't dislike you. He just doesn't want to take the time to work with you. He wants you to work alongside him."

"A peaceful coexistence?" I asked.

"I guess you could call it that," my teacher responded, "though that isn't much help to you in learning the principles behind the experiments, is it?"

Fortunately, I was able to do additional reading and gain much of the required knowledge. The meaning of the experiments was lost for me, thanks, in large part, to a talented young student who had no comprehension what it was like to be legally blind.

The great harm that these people do commit is due to their indifference. Their feelings of apathy are contagious. Instead of making an attempt to work out their feelings, they prefer to close their eyes to the reality of the handicapped. They see no need to learn how to cope with their feelings or how to make contact with the handicapped because they really do not want to have that contact in the first place.

For us this is a particularly difficult reaction to deal with. Do not push for contacts with people like this. Let contact with them come naturally or not at all. To develop a relationship that would have true meaning or depth will be almost impossible.

If you decide that a particular person who holds the "peaceful coexistence" view is so special to you for some other reason that you feel a burning desire to develop a relationship with him, go ahead and try. That is your decision. However, be prepared for disappointment. He may try even harder to ignore you when he becomes aware that you want to develop a relationship. Or he may be so callous as to tell you to "get lost."

Either you will eventually succeed in getting through to him or you will be hurt often enough that you will decide to give up. In either case you will pay a tremendous price in drained emotional energy. If you give up, however, you at least know that someone meant enough to you to make you want to try against great odds to become friends. If you succeed, the joy in this relationship will be unlike any other you have ever known!

An eighth reaction on the part of the general public is that handicapped people always "have their hands out," that they want "something for nothing." This is perhaps one of the most dangerous reactions of all, because people who feel this way are guilty of blatant generalizations that cause them to be angry at "all those handicapped people."

"I had to work hard to get where I am," they say. "Why should someone have everything handed to him on a silver platter by society just because he can't see or hear? It just burns me up!"

You must do your best, first of all, to avoid becoming overly angry at this type of reaction. A bit of anger is understandable, of course, and may lead to constructive action.

People who feel that the handicapped want to have everything handed to them have committed the first injustice by lumping handicapped people into a single category like so many potatoes being dumped into a twenty-pound bag. The generalization is as inaccurate as it is unjust! But beyond that, these people give the handicapped no credit at all for their attempts to work out their own problems.

Such people justify their attitude by saying that they "are only looking out for the public interest." They add that the economy is under great stress and it cannot afford to "let the handicapped make unlimited trips to the public trough."

I remember the day that my counselor from our state agency for the visually impaired came to my home to bring me the new electric typewriter that the state had purchased for my use. I was overjoyed at having a typewriter of my own for my schoolwork and other tasks. But that joy was short-lived when I overheard a neighbor telling someone later that day, "Did you know that that state woman brought her an electric typewriter today? She probably didn't pay a cent for it either. That's why our taxes are going through the roofs! We are expected to provide all the luxuries to those handicapped people so they can live it up!"

I couldn't imagine that this woman would not understand that for someone who has as much trouble with handwriting as I do, a typewriter is a vital means of written communication. Several months afterward I was with this woman in an informal setting and had the opportunity to say something about the incident.

"Well—er," she stammered when I recalled to her what had happened. "We just can't stand the fact that the handicapped always seem to get more out of the government in services than we do. All we do is pay higher and higher taxes!"

"Be glad," I said, "that you don't need these kinds of services. I'd trade places with you any day, but I guess it was intended that you should have perfect vision and that I should not. So I'm willing to accept things as they are."

Do your best to behave in a balanced way with people like this, and above all, don't exhibit anger. For then people might think that you are angry not over the injustice of lumping handicapped people together as "takers" but over the fact that your "handouts" were being threatened. Do not shrug off people like this, but see what you can do to enlarge their view of the world.

Begin by talking about handicapped people you know who are well-adjusted citizens, working productively in their fields of endeavor. It does not matter whether they are factory workers, engineers, secretaries, doctors, or draftsmen. They are hardworking, contributing, taxpaying members of society.

Then speak about the fact that there *are* some handicapped persons who do receive assistance, but the aim of this assistance is to make the handicapped employable, working members of society at whatever their level of capability. Again, this allows the handicapped person to pay taxes and to buy goods and services, just like the vast majority of nonhandicapped Americans.

Several years ago I became acquainted with a prosperous businessman. It was obvious from the day we first met that he had no use for handicapped people. "They always take so long to accomplish anything!" he generalized. "Whatever they can do, a nonhandicapped person could do the same thing in half the time!"

From time to time I cited examples of handicapped people who were accomplishing significant goals. I tried my best to raise these examples at moments when they fit into the discussion as a whole. I avoided making the man feel as though I were talking primarily to him. Still, in spite of my efforts, it seemed as if I were making no progress at all. His comments were just as slanted, his opinions just as strong. A month or two later, however, I learned quite by accident that he had made a sizable tax-deductible contribution to a research center working to eliminate a number of severe birth defects.

Perhaps your contacts with people like my businessman friend will start their thinking processes in the right direction. It may be another person, weeks or even months later, who will reap the benefit of a change in their attitude.

A ninth public reaction is the practice of trying to pigeonhole handicapped persons into a traditional mold. This can be devastating! It is the idea that everyone who is engaged in a particular occupation or activity must do so in only one way.

For instance, such people cannot picture a blind musician, because to them a musician reads his musical notes from the printed page. Since a blind person cannot see, he is to them incapable of being a musician. Never mind the idea that many musicians, sighted or not, memorize their pieces. Or that some talented musicians play by ear, negating the need for reading printed music altogether.

Also, in the area of personnel, the moment an applicant is perceived as being handicapped, the interviewer immediately becomes wary of him. Though the interviewer may have the decency to go through the motions of reviewing his résumé and may even pose a question or two, his mind has been made up from the beginning to disregard this application.

The fact that locating a full-time job is so important to most of us makes these "pigeonholers" all the more a force to be reckoned with and efforts to alter their thinking that much more crucial. They can do irreparable harm to our self-concepts through repeatedly communicating the fact that we are unsuitable for those all-important jobs they have to offer.

But, conversely, if the "pigeonholers" can be made to see the error in their thinking, they can have almost unlimited power to affect us for the better. Such individuals know best of all one word—results. Though they may try diligently to hold fast to their traditional biases about us, they are influenced by concrete evidence to the contrary. A corporate personnel director, for example, will be influenced by a wheelchair-bound factory worker who has demonstrated his ability to produce an amount of goods equal to his ambulatory counterpart.

With these tendencies of employers in mind, be prepared with specific examples and selected facts! When you are granted an interview, go in with the idea that you are going to sell yourself. Your knowledge of that particular business and your conviction that you can handle the particular job will take you a long way. Examples of persons with a similar handicap who are doing the same type of work will carry you even further. Be courteous at all times, but steer the employer away from any generalizations he might make. Guide him instead to the specifics of your particular application. Force him to deal with the facts concerning you as they are, not as he might perceive them to be!

A tenth and final reaction of the general public that we will consider is the exact opposite of the previous reactions. It can best be described as the "superhero" syndrome. Here, every accomplishment of a handicapped person is magnified five, ten, fifteen times over. If a handicapped person receives an award or is successful in obtaining employment, it is a great accomplishment. Anything in which we succeed is automatically labeled "tremendous."

"Isn't she wonderful?," "Isn't he brave?" are comments heard coming from such people. It must be pointed out that they actually believe that we as handicapped people are heroes. They are sincere. In other words, they have perceived to some extent the obstacles that often stand between us and our achievements. To overcome these obstacles, in their view, is not only wonderful but also amazing and worthy of the highest praise.

"So what's wrong with that," you ask. "It *is* a great accomplishment for me to be able to do the things that I do." Indeed it is! What's more, it is refreshing to know that there is a group of people who recognize our achievements as such. But the point is that these people believe the handicapped are heroes instead of simply people trying their best to make productive lives for themselves.

"Then let me be a hero," you say. "At least that's better than being ignored or categorized or 'put away,' which is what some people would like to do to me."

But the danger is that heroes are often a passing fancy, an interesting phenomenon to be admired until something that captivates the people's interest even more comes along. Heroes do not remain heroes forever.

The fact is that we need to be accepted as part of society just as everyone else is. We do not want to be worshiped or adored as heroes any more than we want to be shunned as outcasts or regarded as "God's little mistakes." It is the happy medium for which we are striving. Anything that veers too far to one extreme or the other will hamper our efforts in the long run.

Perhaps the best analogy to consider as we feel overwhelmed by the variety and potential dangers of the public's reactions is to simply turn the tables on the entire situation. In other words, what would it be like for us if the number of nonhandicapped people in the world was much smaller than the number of people with a handicap? What would it be like if, in fact, we were in the majority? Wouldn't we be a bit frightened by the "other kind of people"? Wouldn't it be relatively easy for us at least to try to close our eyes for a while, pretending that nonhandicapped people didn't really exist? Wouldn't we have a tendency to split the world into two categories—"them" and "us"?

This does not mean that we should allow such

prejudicial opinions to be held by the public without doing everything we can to change those opinions. What it does mean is that we must attain a level of tolerance for the fears and insecurities that serve as a breeding ground for the prejudices and injustices that result.

On the positive side, remember that there are many people who sincerely want to understand our problems—and to help us—if they only knew how. I have been encouraged by many such people, who tell me that it is very useful for them to hear about the problems of the handicapped from someone who truly *is* handicapped. They do not want to listen to a scholar, qualified as he may be, who has studied the problems of the handicapped and is advocating academically based solutions.

Begin now! Get in there and do your part! Fight with the best weapons you have—understanding, examples, facts, and an abiding desire to see the world become a better place in which to live— for "them" and for "us"—for everyone!

EIGHT

Motivate Yourself!

In the first part of this book we looked at six basic problem areas affecting nearly everyone who is handicapped. As we discussed each problem, we also offered solutions for dealing with it. However, something more is necessary to ensure that you lead a fulfilling life, and that is a healthy general attitude. Therefore, we will now look in detail at four fundamental ingredients that make up this attitude—the ability to motivate yourself, to think positively, to approach your life realistically, and to be at peace with yourself.

Whether we are aware of it or not, motivation plays an important part in almost everything we do. We are motivated to get up in the morning, to accomplish specific tasks within a given day, to pay our bills on time, and a host of other routine matters. For some people, motivating themselves to perform these routine tasks is as far as it goes. But for you as a handicapped person this is not nearly enough! Your motivation must carry you a great deal further!

The dictionary defines motivation as "a need or a desire that causes a person to act." Because you are handicapped, it may take you twice as long to accomplish something or you may have to exert twice as much effort to achieve a specific goal. Therefore, this desire must burn inside you like an eternal flame that is constant and glowing! Without this flame you will be hard-pressed to exert the often herculean effort required for you to "get the job done"—whatever that job may be.

The necessity for this almost superhuman effort was brought home to me vividly when my dearest friend required my help following surgery. To minimize the risk of infection, the doctors determined that she should be sent home with an open incision and allow it to heal gradually from the inside out. This meant that three times daily I would have to change the dressing that covered the incision. Each time, all steps for a sterile procedure had to be followed. This included scrubbing my arms to the elbows and following explicit directions. At first, knowing that there were so many danger signs to look for as well as numerous possibilities for error, I felt it was more than I could handle. I panicked at the thought of everything that could go wrong!

Later that day the doctor told us that if someone could not be found to do the dressings, my friend would have to go to a nursing home where she could receive the necessary care. Faced with that as the only alternative, I decided to give it a try. For her, fear of nursing home placement was matched only by our commitment to avoid it. Perspiration dripped off me and every muscle in my body grew tense as I began to learn the procedure under the watchful eye of wonderful nurses. The first time or two I literally collapsed on the nearby cot when the procedure was finished. I had never tried so hard to accomplish anything in all my life! But gradually it got easier. Although there was always a certain tension while I was performing the procedure, I reminded myself constantly *why* I was doing this. Without that strong sense of motivation, I am convinced that I could never have managed to keep this up for the necessary ten weeks.

I learned a valuable lesson from this experience. Although I was terrified at the time, the fact that I could motivate myself sufficiently to do what needed to be done did a great deal to bolster my self confidence. Now I feel as though I could meet the challenge of almost any task as long as my motivation never wavered!

Once you possess this strong motivation, nothing that requires a hundred percent commitment from you will be beyond your grasp! You will have what it takes to stick with a particular task until it is successfully completed.

Since motivation is so crucial to your living a fulfilling life, how then do you acquire this motivation? Four things are necessary to obtain it, and they all come from within. There is only one person who can motivate you for any length of time—you yourself. Other people may be able to "psych you up" for a specific event the way fans psych up members of a basketball team before the "big game." Or they may be able to motivate you to accomplish a specific task, such as making a speech before a large audience. But in the long run you have the responsibility for motivating yourself. Only you can determine what is important to you. You must decide the goals for which you are willing to make sacrifices and then strive to attain them!

The first component in achieving self-motivation is to have a strong sense of direction. You must know what your aim is. You cannot simply say, "I have to motivate myself!" without asking the all-important question "For what?"

As you seek this goal, realize that if you choose one that is too far in the future, your motivation will lose its strength because you see few, if any, results on a day-to-day basis. You have no yard-stick with which to measure your progress. When you are unsure of how well you are doing, it is far too easy to become disheartened and give up.

On the other hand, you must guard against setting too many short-range goals. For when this happens, the goal is attained so rapidly that it does not provide a continued stimulus for your motivation. When you do set short-range goals, be prepared to replace them frequently so that your motivation will remain strong.

The solution, then, as is so often the case, is to strike a happy medium, with a combination of short- and long-range goals. In this way, the long-range goals will provide a sustained sense of direction, while the short-range goals will give you a sufficient sense of achievement to make you want to continue to strive onward.

The second component in achieving self motivation is to decide upon a goal that is "right." You may ask, "How do I know whether it is 'right' or not?" Quite simply, it must be "right" for you. That is, it must fit in with your overall system of values and priorities.

For example, a well-planned long-range goal for you might be to develop your own stamp collection. But if you do not enjoy going through stamp catalogs, attending collectors' shows, and mounting the stamps once you get them, then this is the wrong goal for you. If, instead, you enjoy buying old pieces of furniture and refinishing them, then perhaps your goal might be to re-decorate an entire room using only antique furniture.

In other words, choose a goal that fits your needs. Do not choose a specific goal because a friend suggests it or because you think that "everybody's doing it." These are poor reasons for selecting a goal. Motivation to accomplish a goal chosen in this way will not remain strong. Chances are you will not succeed, because such a goal was not "right" for you in the first place.

A friend of mine decided one day that she wanted to learn how to ice skate. Because I valued her friendship, enjoyed being with her, and wanted to be able to spend more time together, I decided that I should learn how to ice skate too. My choice of this goal was entirely wrong, because it did not meet my needs. I did not have the necessary vision or coordination to ice skate. I had no genuine desire to learn how to skate. In fact, I loathed the thought of it as the time drew near for our first lesson. Fortunately, I came to my senses and realized my mistake before anything dangerous took place. And, as for my desire to spend more time together with my friend, it was accomplished by going to see plays instead. This was much more realistic and an activity we both enjoyed.

To be right, a goal must be in line with your system of values. That is, it must not conflict with anything that you believe in strongly. It must also correspond to your interests, the limitations imposed by your handicap, and your financial constraints. Test the goal you are considering by applying one or all of these criteria. If your goal conforms, you can be relatively certain that it is the right goal for you.

The third component to achieving self motivation is to develop the ability to set limits for yourself. You cannot possibly motivate yourself to work on five or six goals at one time, so don't set that many. If you try, you will find that you run out of steam, your motivation weakens, and you will become needlessly discouraged.

Instead, select one or two major goals that you believe are of the greatest importance to your living a fulfilling life. Make one a short-range goal, the other a long-range goal. Then push full steam ahead with these specific goals. In this way your energies will not become fragmented. You will be able to move ahead with gusto!

You must apply the same techniques to your minor goals. Since they are smaller in nature and will probably require less time to complete, it is easy to plan too many of them for yourself, thinking that you will be able to fit them all into your schedule. This can be just as frustrating as having too many long-range goals. So guard against too many such involvements.

Nearly every one of us has come into contact with a person who says yes with enthusiasm to everything that he is asked to do. At first it may appear that this individual is truly wonderful for consenting to do so much. This feeling of admiration for his willingness soon wears thin, however, when it becomes apparent that he cannot get everything done in a timely manner. He did not want to disappoint anyone, but he disappoints them far more by not doing as he promised than he would have by saying in the first place, "No, I'm sorry. Not this time." How much better it would have been for his own peace of mind and for that of his colleagues if he had said yes to just one or two things, completed them successfully, and declined the other tasks.

The fourth component is to be flexible. If all your energies are directed toward one or two goals and then, for some reason, it becomes obvious that one or the other goal cannot be attained, you must be flexible. You must be willing to change your direction in these instances and pursue your newly chosen course with an equal amount of vim and vigor!

As a youngster, when the time came to select a musical instrument to play, I had my heart set on playing the viola. My sister had taken up the violin several years before, and I marveled at her ability to draw the bow across the strings and produce such beautiful tones. When my turn came, I wanted to play a stringed instrument also and had settled on the viola.

I had a private teacher who spent a good number of hours trying to get my fingers to perform properly. A certain dexterity was required to use the bow while at the same time holding the instrument itself in a steady manner. Try as I would, I did not have the coordination to combine these two processes. Either the hand that held the bow would tremble so that the sound had a muddy quality or I would be unable to hold the viola itself in the proper way.

One day, when the instructor could stand my feeble attempts no longer, he said, "Gillian, you try so hard! I wish all my students would try as hard as you do. But it's no use. You simply cannot learn to play the viola!" And to add insult to injury, he said, "And I must spend my time teaching students who have talent, not just the desire to learn." He was right, of course, but I felt as though my world had collapsed. Not play the viola! Why, someone could have said, "Cut off your head!" and I would have been no less crushed.

For several days I could think of nothing but all the concerts I would not be able to participate in and the fact that my sister and I would now be unable to play duets together—something I had looked forward to most of all. The following week, fortunately for me, our school was recruiting woodwind players for both band and orchestra. This family of instruments was a more realistic choice, since only one set of finger motions was required to play them successfully. After a demonstration by one of our band directors, I knew I had found my instrument. The clarinet, also known as the violin of the woodwind family, would be my choice.

Though the sting of my failure to play the viola wore off very slowly, I was now able to channel my energies to a new, more attainable goal. The concerts, solo, and duet opportunities came along in time also. And the satisfaction of playing an instrument was genuine and lasting!

A person who lacks flexibility is likely to be miserable every time he finds he cannot achieve the goal he had originally established. He will be unhappy and dissatisfied within himself. What is more, he will be unwilling to find a new area to which he can direct his energies.

There are, then, four components necessary for you to motivate yourself. Each is much like a piece of a jigsaw puzzle. If you have only one or two pieces, you will never be able to put the puzzle together. But combine all of them and you will have a beautiful picture! By utilizing the four components we have discussed, you will be able to generate sufficient motivational energy to achieve almost any goal!

Earlier we said there is only one person—you yourself—who can motivate you for any length of time. This is very true. However, this does not mean that another person, probably a family member or a friend, cannot provide limited help to you when your motivation may be faltering.

Perhaps you have had a particularly disappointing experience or you have found that one of your goals must be adjusted. While you *will* overcome these obstacles, it is natural to feel a bit down in the dumps during those times. A friend or family member may be able to offer just the shot in the arm you need to bolster your morale and return your motivation to its previous level. This support may come in the form of a diversion, such as a few days of vacation, or it could be simply the opportunity to talk things out in a pleasant environment at an unhurried pace.

Do not hesitate to call on someone occasionally to help strengthen you when the need arises. Chances are, knowing how diligently you have worked toward various goals you set for yourself in the past, people will be happy to be supportive of you when you need them.

If your resolve is sagging a bit, you may also find it beneficial to turn your thoughts away from the situation for a time. Use this break to help another person in some *special* way. It is remarkable what a little change of emphasis can do to lift your spirits.

During a particularly heavy week, when my work seemed to be piling up at an alarming rate, I suddenly decided that I had to break away from my efforts or risk becoming overwhelmed and discouraged. An elderly lady who was very close to me had been urging me to come for a visit. A perfect solution! For several hours one afternoon I thoroughly enjoyed myself by looking at her family picture albums with her and hearing about working conditions when she was employed years ago in her native England. We even baked a batch of molasses cookies!

I returned home wondering why I hadn't thought to do this several days before. The next day I approached my work with a renewed sense of purpose and a generally happier disposition.

When you detect that your motivation is on the decline, do not hesitate to take action as I did and do something about it right away! Try pursuing an activity that is soothing to you, such as listening to music or taking a ride in the country. Whatever your choice, for it to be effective be sure that it requires use of your sensory perceptions or other physical skills rather than a great deal of mental exertion. While you are relaxed, let your mind wander. Imagine yourself at a particular location that you like. Dream a little bit. You will soon find that your mind has been refreshed and you will feel ready to go back to your more pressing tasks.

Above all, pray about it. Explain the entire situation to God. Pray in the way that is most comfortable to you. Your prayer may take the form of a letter that you might be writing to a friend. This is appropriate, for He is the dearest Friend that you have! Do not hold anything back. If you are having problems, tell Him about them. Be specific. "Discuss" it openly. Remember that God is the perfect listener. In His infinite patience, He will hear you out completely. Just the fact that you are able to unburden yourself to Him will have a positive effect. When we are at our best, it is quite simple to be cheery, energetic, and enthusiastic. But when we feel overburdened or discouraged, isn't it wonderful to be able to turn to Someone who will help us?

As you pray, keep an open mind. Be receptive to the thoughts that flow in ever so gently. They may result in your feeling a renewed sense of purpose. God desires that His children find meaning in their lives. Through a strong sense of motivation and specific goals, you too will find this meaning. It is waiting for you!

NINE

Be Positive!

Approach your life optimistically! Although this is far easier said than done, a positive outlook is the second fundamental ingredient that contributes to a healthy general attitude. Next to a strong God-centered faith, there is nothing more important than a positive approach to life. It can make all the difference in the world between success and failure, between your being happy and being miserable.

Thinking positively is essential to your living a fulfilling life. In this chapter we will discuss five aspects of your positive approach to living—being positive about yourself, your relationships with other people, the situations that confront you in daily living, your future, and your relationship with God.

The first aspect, then, is to be positive about yourself. This must begin with you before you can extend it to others!

I remember a particular spelling bee at school. When the competition was announced, it was as if a firecracker exploded inside me. "Here's something I can compete in with the same chance to succeed as everyone else!" I thought.

And, true enough, vision was not to play a part in the contest. The teacher would announce the word. We were to repeat it and then spell it. For days I could think of little else. The possibility of participating in *and winning* something competitive was strange and unfamiliar to me.

The day of the spelling bee I awakened with a surge of energy quite different from other mornings, when getting up was merely routine. All through the day I felt a burning desire to compete. As the competition began, the easier words came first and then the more challenging ones. One by one I saw my classmates falter and take their seats, looking more than a little dejected. But I continued. Soon there were only two of us remaining. Furious was the next word on the list. "F-u-r-i-o-s," my opponent spelled slowly. Scarcely able to contain my joy, I quieted down, outwardly at least, and spelled the word correctly. The prize of a small chocolate candy bar could not have meant more to me if it had been a diamond-studded necklace or a trip around the world. I had set my mind on something and I had won!

There is no doubt that when the time came for the next spelling bee I could approach it in a healthy, positive manner. Whether I won or not was now unimportant. For I had proven to myself that by carefully choosing an important goal that was right for me, and approaching it positively, I could succeed.

Taking the positive approach to something as small as a spelling bee does not seem very significant when compared to the major decisions we must make throughout our lifetime. What makes it significant, however, is that it begins to set a pattern for the future. Begin thinking in this way about the little things, and it will become that much easier to face the bigger things.

You must be positive when you look at yourself. "What do you like about yourself?" Think about it. Making a list on a sheet of paper in your notebook will be helpful. Your list may be slow in forming, but each addition to it will improve your self concept. As you think along this line, you may even come up with characteristics that describe you that you had never thought of before.

Enlist the help of other people who know you well as you are making this list. They can tell you what they like most about you as a person. They may also mention a fault or two of yours that is particularly annoying to them. But if that happens, welcome it. Look upon it as an opportunity to learn where your weaknesses are and then think about the ways you can improve. Thinking about your faults is also positive, though somewhat less pleasant, because it means that you are trying to improve yourself.

Strange as it may seem, you may even find some positive aspects about your handicap that you had never considered before. When I mentioned to a good friend of mine the fact that I was only partially sighted, she responded, "Yes, but not being able to see well makes you use your sense of hearing more. You hear things that I often miss!" Strange, but I had never considered that before. She was right. Since my eyes provide only limited sight, my ears compensate for the loss. A person who is fully sighted might take his sight, hearing, and other sensory skills for granted. But I am at an advantage there because I am not likely to do so. Each sight I see, each sound I hear, has a special meaning to me.

An even more important positive aspect of your handicap is that it may make you more understanding and more tolerant of others. That is a quality that many people have to work to develop, but yours may come almost naturally, because you have had understanding extended to you by others for many years. And often the easiest way to learn such a quality is by example. Almost unknowingly, you may have gained a valuable character trait that will make you a good business associate and a good friend.

There are many other positive traits you will find as you look at the person you are. The more you explore these positive traits, the more you will see that like most people, you have many good qualities.

The beauty of being positive about yourself is that it is contagious. The power of this kind of thinking is endless. When we take the focus away from ourselves and turn it in other directions, this same spirit permeates our thinking.

The second aspect is to be positive about your relationships with other people. This is not difficult to do with members of your family and your friends. You are well aware of what it is that makes these persons very special to you. You have known and loved them for years. The difficulty comes, however, with persons whom you do not love so much, and particularly with those whom you find it difficult to deal with effectively.

Remember, though, even they have endearing qualities. If you adopt a positive approach to them, you will see favorable results soon. In many instances the very people who seem unfriendly or difficult to work with are the ones who have a negative self concept. They are filled with feelings of inadequacy and weakness. These feelings spill over into their dealings with you. Keep in mind that these people do not mean to be un-friendly to you personally, although it may seem that way to you.

A counselor I was assigned to in high school is a perfect illustration of this. Every time he talked with me, I had the feeling that he really didn't want to be bothered, that he would rather be doing something else or talking with someone else. When he had a piece of information to share with me, he would preface his remarks with "I don't think you'll be interested in this, but . . . " I had a negative feeling before he even got to the heart of what he wanted to share with me. After a while his negative approach began to disturb me.

Soon after that I spoke with another counselor about the problem in the hope of finding out what I had done wrong. She reassured me that I had done nothing wrong and proceeded to tell me confidentially that this man was having family problems. He was suffering under the burden of them and was unable to pull his life together. Therefore, he was taking a negative approach to everyone and everything. Even when something good *did* come his way, he was immediately suspicious that it was a mistake or that something had been "rigged."

After I understood more about this unhappy counselor, I would go out of my way to share positive things with him. When I achieved something worthwhile, I would tell him about it in a way that made him feel that he had a part in it. He didn't change overnight, of course, but after a time he would speak to me first when we saw each other in the hallway. And occasionally he would even smile!

You too can be of great help to the people you know by showing your positive attitude. Naturally, you hope that they will extend the same to you, but even when that does not happen you can feel happy inside that you were able to brighten their day, and maybe even to improve their outlook a little.

As you strive to feel positive in your relationships with other people, it is also important to have such feelings when you meet people for the first time. When you meet a stranger, remember that he may feel uncomfortable. There is a certain amount of apprehension anytime two strangers meet. "Will I make a good first impression?" "Will I say the right things?" "Will the other person like me?"

These feelings of uncertainty are often compounded when one of the strangers is handicapped. As we discussed earlier, the other person may not know how to approach you because of your handicap. One of my friends said, "These braces ᴅo funny things to people," referring to the braces on his legs that made it possible for him to walk.

In a situation like this, your attitude can make a world of difference. A smile and a friendly hello is the world's best icebreaker when you are introduced. Immediately, the other person sees someone who is friendly and at ease. You have gotten your first encounter with this stranger off to a flying start!

The third aspect is to be positive about the situations that confront you in daily living. If you try hard enough, you can find a positive approach to almost any situation, though sometimes you may have to look very hard before you find it.

A friend once told me about how she would always feel faint at the sight of blood. While she didn't actually faint, she would become ill when she saw blood. A small cut on her finger could produce this effect almost as readily as if she saw a pool of blood.

Then one day her uncle needed surgery. He told her that if in the course of surgery he would need a blood transfusion, fresh blood would be available to replenish what he had lost. "Someone had to be willing to donate that blood," he explained. "I feel good knowing that it will be there in readiness if I need it."

My friend admitted that she had never before thought of blood as being a life-giving substance. She had always associated blood with injuries and serious medical problems. Her attitude changed dramatically. In fact, sometime later she even signed up to be a donor at her local blood bank.

What made the difference for my friend? The substance of blood was the same. It was her attitude that had changed. She turned a negative feeling into a positive approach and did something constructive about it.

The same can be said of you as a handicapped person. Your handicap remains constant. In all likelihood it will be with you always. It affects many phases of your life. These facts, like the substance of blood, will not change. What makes the difference is *your* attitude. If it is negative, your attitude will darken every situation that confronts you. But if it is positive, you will have an edge on whatever the circumstance may be. You can see yourself as a "cripple" or as a "fighter." The handicap that you have will be there regardless of which position you adopt. But you can do a great deal to change what effect it has on you.

The situations that confront you in daily living can change dramatically from day to day or even from hour to hour. Because of the volatile nature of anyone's life, a positive attitude becomes that much more important. For example, from one day to the next you might lose your job or suffer a setback in your medical condition. No one welcomes such changes, of course, but if you have nurtured a positive approach to living, these changes will have a far less devastating effect upon you. They may still shock you, anger you somewhat, and cause you to feel depressed for a time, but they will not destroy you!

After college graduation a friend and I worked for nearly a year and a half to establish a twenty-four-hour-a-day, seven-day-a-week information, referral, and crisis hotline. We set up the nonprofit corporation with the help of other community people and obtained the funding to operate the program for its first year. After that time additional funding was granted, and we believed that it would continue indefinitely. We handled all types of questions, problems, and needs from the sixty thousand–plus residents of our county.

My job as an information specialist was ideal because I was able to use my skills in communication. The need for visual acuity was limited. Our call volume soared. Month after month the statistics as well as the complexity of the calls would increase. We were on top of the world!

But as time went on it became all too obvious that the initial funding for the program was drying up, while long-term funding sources in the wake of a tightening economy were nowhere to be found. Solely due to lack of financial backing, the program was terminated.

For a time I felt as though the bottom had dropped out of not only my career, but my world. We had worked so hard, only to end in defeat! What's more, the people who used our service so regularly now would suffer because there was nothing with which it would be replaced. I was in despair.

But my despair did not last long. Slowly, my friend and I began to make new plans. Our spirits began to reassert themselves. The further along our plans for the future developed, the higher our spirits rose. Though we still feel a tinge of sadness at the demise of our program that would never be, we were able to take the good from it and discard the rest.

Remember as you are working to develop a positive approach to the situations that confront you that God intends each of His children to view his life in a positive way. He does not expect you to live with a negative frame of mind. True, everyone has negative thoughts at one time or another, but a positive attitude will help you rise above them.

Although it happened a number of years ago, I remember my futile efforts at obtaining a job on the staff of a particular newspaper. The man who was interviewing for the position was well pleased with my qualifications for the position and said that he was sure "something mutually satisfactory to both of us" could be worked out.

At the end of the interview I told him that I felt it only right for him to know about my sight problem. I presented it factually but with a decidedly positive approach, including an explanation of how I planned to cope with my transportation needs.

Although he had already placed a copy of the newspaper's employee contract on his desk toward me, he said, "Well, perhaps we had better think this over a bit," while discreetly pulling the papers back toward himself.

Needless to say, I never heard from him again. For a few days I was certain that he would call. But as one week melted into another I could deceive myself no longer. My handicap had frightened him away. He was unwilling to give me a chance or to give himself the opportunity to see what I could do.

Once again my positive attitude rose to the surface in spite of the fact that I was much tempted to question my self worth. After all, if I was not suitable for a job that stressed writing and communications skills, and this was one of my major areas of study, then what good would I be? I soon realized that such thinking could only lead me down a dead-end street. Only a complete turnaround in my approach could bring positive results. And that is exactly what I did! And it wasn't long before I knew that one door does not close unless another one opens.

The fourth aspect is to be positive about your future. Your future and the anticipation of it is a gift to you from God. You must view each day as an opportunity all its own—first of all, to improve you own situation, and then to help others as best you can.

Though the present circumstances of your life may give the impression of a dismal future, do not dwell on them. Face them squarely, do what you can to improve them, and go on. Shift your focus to other aspects of your life that will provide meaning and offer challenges to you.

As I was completing high school, two areas of my life began to bother me greatly. One was that nagging problem of my inability to drive, and the other was the problem of functioning alone in unfamiliar territory, particularly in large cities, without posing a real and present danger to myself. My lack of vision and coordination made navigating in strange surroundings exceptionally difficult despite the fact that I was nearly an adult.

For some time I had been unusually depressed. At first, I ignored these feelings, but eventually my depression forced me to come to grips with the cause of those feelings. It didn't take long to isolate the problem or the facts surrounding it. I saw my friends growing up in these two important areas while I lagged miserably behind. The future did not hold much promise in either area, since neither my chances for driving nor my visual acuity and coordination were destined to change.

Even after isolating the cause of my depression I brooded. "Why me?" kept sounding in my mind and then "My future looks bleak."

Eventually my friends began to notice the change in my outlook. "Come on, Gillian. Get with it!" they said. "We're almost out of high school. College is ahead. Isn't it great?" I was torn in two directions. Of course, the thought of high school graduation and college was exciting. Still, I could not bring myself to be optimistic with the problems that hung above me like an ominous black thundercloud.

One day one of them cornered me after school and suggested that we walk home instead of taking the bus. "This is ridiculous, Gillian!" she said. "You've got to snap out of this! You're making yourself and those around you miserable. That's not like you!"

She was right! I was making other people unhappy, and I certainly wasn't helping myself any either. What to do? That night I sat in my room with a blank sheet of paper on my desk in front of me. Slowly, in bold red pen, I wrote PROBLEMS and drew a line down the center of the page. On the other side of the line I wrote the word SOLUTIONS. I listed the problems as I saw them. That certainly didn't take long, though just the process of writing them down seemed to remove them from my brain, where they were getting all muddled up. It brought them out into the open, where they could be dealt with more easily. After that I didn't write anything for more than an hour. I didn't move from my chair, but I certainly did a lot of thinking! I looked at possible solutions. Some I discarded instantly as being unworkable. Others were tossed out after a little more thought. But a few remained. Those solutions that seemed the most workable eventually were written under the SOLUTIONS column opposite the appropriate problem. For example, on the driving issue I wrote, "Offer to type term papers for someone in exchange for rides."

The specific solutions, such as paying someone to drive me, were not nearly as important as the fact that I had stopped emoting and started thinking. At last I was beginning to deal with the problems concerning my future.

What's more, when I had done as much as I could that night, I turned my thoughts to the debate tournament in which I was to compete that weekend—away from my problems and toward something bright and challenging.

Do not allow concern for your future to blind you to what joys may be yours in the present. Take the good that each day has to offer! When you do think ahead, consider only one area of your life at a time. Allow yourself to look to the future only as long as there are constructive actions you can take now to improve it. Your future will be as bright as you make it! Approach it positively!

The fifth aspect is to be positive in your relationship with God. If you are, you will draw the maximum amount of strength from His love and guidance. God loves you and has a concern for you both now and in the future. It would be very easy for you to think, "God doesn't want to be bothered with my problems. He's too busy helping our world leaders who are praying for peace or helping a part of the world that is ravaged by disaster." This is a negative thought. Wipe it out of your mind! Nothing could be further from the truth.

Instead, think of God as a concerned Friend who is willing to listen at any time and hear about anything. No problem is too small if it is your problem. No problem is too great if it is your problem. Carry your burdensome concerns to Him and He will guide you through them. Not rapidly, perhaps. He may not work an instant solution or even a solution at all as you and I would think of it. But He will help you to clarify the situation in a manner that will make your next step clear.

Remember as a little child when you were bullied at school or when someone poked fun at you because you were different from them in some way? When you came home in the afternoon and spilled out what had happened, often with one word tumbling upon the next between stifled sobs, you felt better just from the act of sharing it with your parents, who cared. They did not ignore you but instead listened patiently to every detail. It is the same with God—now and always.

Perhaps more than any other illustration, my concept of God was changed dramatically from a punishing God to that of a loving God by a friend who reminded me that "God in heaven is very much like your father here on earth. Both of them care about you now and will continue to care about you in the future."

With that single analogy God became a positive force in my life because my father has always been my greatest friend, supporter, disciplinarian, and confidant. Whenever anything was wrong, I would wait eagerly for the moment when I could share it with him. He was always willing to listen and ready to advise gently, guiding firmly only when necessary. Even as I mature over the years, his opinions remain important to me.

Another aspect of the relationship I have with my father helps me to understand the potential of a positive relationship with God. My father is always kind and loving even when I do something that is not to his liking. He does not like what I have done always, but this does not mean that he loves me as his child any less. It is much the same with God. He may not approve of all your actions on earth, but He still loves you as His most special child. Because of the strength of that love, He is willing to take the time to guide you if you will but listen to Him and practice in your daily life what He tells you.

Whether it is a parent, spouse, or friend, it is helpful to liken God's love for you to a person on earth who exhibits a deep love for you. It is then easy to comprehend the depth of God's love that creates the potential for the most positive relationship of all—the relationship between you and your God.

Be positive that God is there for you even if you have turned away from Him at other times in your life. Be positive that He will forgive those acts you have committed that cause you anguish or unhappiness if you will pray for that forgiveness. Be positive that He will stand beside you at all times in your life—the good times as well as the trying times. And, above all, believe that as your relationship with God grows, as you become more comfortable with the role He plays in your life, you will become a happier, more positive-thinking person leading a more fulfilling life.

God is positive that you are a uniquely beautiful part of His human creation. You must be positive that He will forever be the guiding light in your life.

TEN

Be Realistic!

Approach your life realistically! This is the third fundamental ingredient aimed at composing a healthy general attitude. And it is this attitude that will contribute to your living a fulfilling life in spite of your handicap!

Have you ever awakened from a deep sleep in which you were dreaming a particularly happy dream? You had to jar yourself into realizing that indeed what you were experiencing *was* only a dream. Or perhaps you expressed some ideas to a close friend about just how you would like things to be, and that friend's reaction was "Wake up! You're in the real world now!"

Both of these experiences serve to remind us that the world we live in is not a utopia where everything is just the way we would like it to be. There is indeed a sharp contrast between the world as we would envision it and the world as it actually exists. To be successful, we must live in the world as it is. There is credence to the argument that this is especially true for handicapped persons. We would like to believe, for example, that our opportunities in the key areas of employment and housing are equal to everyone else's. But in reality we know that we must try twice as hard if we are to win these opportunities. And even then we will not always be successful.

Therefore, the first aspect of approaching your life realistically is to begin with yourself. While you may wish with all your heart that you had two sound legs, or two eyes that focused together, or fingers that responded when you wanted them to, the fact is that you don't. Somewhere, somehow, something caused you to be handicapped, and a little different from other people. Realizing the truth in that statement is part of what we mean by being realistic about yourself.

But as you look at yourself, being realistic means much more than that. It means putting your handicap into perspective—understanding and living within your limitations. There was a time when I wanted to learn very much how to sew. I had heard my friends talk about sewing and had seen the finished products they made—party dresses, tailored suits, robes, and more. The clothes were pretty and could be made at a fraction of the cost that I had to pay to buy them at a store. Ignoring the reality of my handicap, one day I made up my mind that I was going to learn to sew. But it was a hopeless task.

To begin with, I could not see the material clearly enough to know where to stitch. I was unable to coordinate hand and eye motions to guide the sewing machine effectively. My father pointed out that in addition, it was dangerous, since the machine had moving parts and I could easily injure myself. In short, the idea of learning to sew with my particular handicap was not only unwise but totally unrealistic.

For weeks thereafter I bemoaned the fact that I did not have a hobby like so many of my friends. What made me even more unhappy was that I had nothing constructive to do when I wasn't studying. Then something very special happened. A teacher of mine who remains today one of my very dearest friends was teaching a course in the evenings entitled "How to Cane a Chair." Although I had never been one to truly appreciate caned furniture, I did like the finished product. What is more, I had read accounts of totally blind people who had learned the craft through a finely developed sense of touch. So I knew that this could be a realistic hobby for me.

I enrolled in the class and had the time of my life! It was a small group of perhaps seven or eight people. Much personal attention was given to each participant as we worked on our individual chairs. I had also enjoyed the experience of going to the flea market and selecting just the chair I wanted. It became an object of personal pride for me. I was determined to cane that chair as carefully as I knew how.

Of course, there were problems. The long strands of cane would twist at times as I tried to weave them into the pattern. To compensate for that, I learned to feel the shiny side as opposed to the dull side. Whenever I was unsure if the strand was twisted, I ran my finger up and down it, using my sense of touch instead of sight to give me the answer. I daresay that overcoming that obstacle and others like it took extra patience on my instructor's part as she worked with me. But there is also no doubt that on the last night of the course, when each of us displayed our finished product, she felt an even greater sense of pride as she passed my chair, with its seat woven evenly and strongly.

Very often people believe that being realistic means facing up to all of the things which they *can't* do, the dreams that can't be fulfilled, the opportunities that can't be met. They view realism as something negative, which means denying themselves at least some of the hidden desires of the heart.

As a start toward looking at yourself realistically, concentrate on what you *can* do. Explore various ways to use the talents that you do have. Don't limit yourself simply because you have not considered every avenue that is open to you. Even if something seems farfetched at first, do not discard it as an option until you have examined it thoroughly. Only then are you truly in a position to make a decision as to whether or not that particular option is right for you.

Now move on and use the same rules as you consider the type of work you want to do to earn a living. Instead of limiting yourself and considering only a few job areas, take a look at the wide range of possibilities. You need to go deeper than simply saying, for example, "I can't be an architect, but I'd like to be a lawyer or a writer." You should first fully explore those skills that come naturally to you, and then look at the occupations that require those skills. You should not begin by saying, "I want to be an accountant," but instead, "I can work with figures and I pay close attention to details. Where can I best use these skills?"

When you look at your skills, you will see that a realistic assessment still provides you with many options. As a mathematician, for example, you can look to careers in industry, education, computers, business, and myriad other areas. Or it may be a combination of these fields that will eventually lead you to the right job choice.

Remember too that there are an infinite number

of variations even within a single occupation. In the field of medicine, for example, a physician who diagnoses illnesses in his patients and then refers them to a specialist will probably never see the sight of an operating room. Similarly, an attorney who deals in corporate law, negotiating contracts, is likely never to see a juvenile courtroom.

The second aspect is to be realistic about your relationships with other people, especially when you go for an interview.

In one interview the employer asked me how I ever adjusted to being legally blind. He said, "I use my eyes for everything. I couldn't function at all if I didn't have my sight." Obviously, this gentleman had never had much contact with partially sighted people, since he could not even understand how we functioned, let alone held down jobs.

I explained to him that I had been legally blind since the age of five months and that, as a result, I had never known life any other way. Then I went on to tell him that I had always compensated as much as possible for my lack of sight with other senses. I wanted to help him see that there were ways of dealing with the problem. It did not mean that the world had come to a screeching halt!

As we talked further, this man showed an increasing amount of amazement at what I was saying. It was as if he did not know, until that moment, that a person could function with very little sight. He needed to be shown, to see and hear for himself. My conversation with that gentleman did not cause a change in his attitude for a long time. In fact, the next time after our first interview, when he had a job opening, he clearly did not consider me a viable candidate, although he went through the motions of interviewing me again. Some months later when a similar opening came up, he reviewed my credentials for the third time. Then, recalling my enthusiasm, he interviewed me again—seriously this time. His attitude had changed. "You just didn't give up, did you?" he said to me that day. "What made you keep on hoping after I discouraged you so strongly?"

"I believed I could do the job," I replied. "It was just a matter of convincing *you* that I could do it."

In your relationships with nonhandicapped people you must also remember that they may be using their emotions rather than their intellect. Realistically, when they give it some thought, they realize that a handicapped person can indeed perform specific jobs in which their handicap would play little or no part at all. But instead, they conjure up images of the "poor little soul" who cannot function on his own and is totally dependent upon society for his every need. Of course, it is easier for the nonhandicapped person to deal with the image of us that he has held for so long than to be brave enough to change his mind! By looking at all of us as totally handicapped persons, he reinforces his belief that we will certainly not express interest in jobs or organizations wherein we would come in contact with "normal" people.

A school principal whom I knew showed utter amazement when told that a young girl with a hearing impairment wanted to participate in a regular school sport. "Why, she would have enough trouble just keeping up with her routine schoolwork!" he said. "How could she even think about competing in an extra-curricular activity?" Once again, this gentleman had an image of a struggling young girl who could barely keep herself afloat academically. It was beyond his comprehension why she would ever want to add another area of "frustration" to her life.

What he failed to understand was that in the first place, the student did quite well in her schoolwork. She had mastered the lip-reading technique very well and was thus able to understand what was being said by her teachers and classmates. In addition, it was very important for her to find an area of competition where her hearing deficiency would not be a major factor. There was nothing wrong with her arms and legs. In fact, the success she might experience in sports would probably carry over to her attitude about school in general. She could then decide to try even harder in the areas where she *did* have difficulty.

In this way, her overall scholastic experience would become a more positive one.

Finally, in your relationships with nonhandicapped people remember that it is difficult at first for them to look at you in a realistic way. Much of the materials that people read or the stories they see on television compound this problem. The media portray handicapped people who make successes of their lives as the exception. The general public hears about a handicapped person who was able to adapt an apartment to his physical limitations or one who worked at a job never held before by someone with a handicap and made a success of it. This reinforces the public's belief that such things happen rarely and are not the norm.

You can expect, however, that nonhandicapped people will exercise genuine effort to become accustomed to us as contributing members of society. You must believe that the more positive experiences you have and the more you share these experiences with others, the more people will come to realize how great our potential really is!

The third aspect is to be realistic about the situations that confront you in daily living. This means taking time to analyze situations carefully rather than jumping immediately to conclusions. What is really involved in the particular situation? How much of a role will my limitations play? What can I do to adjust the situation to fit my needs better? You must ask yourself these and other questions every time a new challenge comes your way. These questions cannot be answered in a minute or perhaps even in an hour. But a better understanding of the answers will ensure more intelligent reactions to each situation.

As a youngster I was very eager to become a Girl Scout. The meetings of the group were held at a little church about four or five blocks from my elementary school. When I first learned where the meetings would be, I almost decided not to join. My reasoning seemed clear at the time. Although we would be driven home after the meetings, we were expected to walk to the church on our own. The path to the church was unfamiliar to me. I was afraid of getting lost. What is more, there were two heavily traveled streets to cross, and I was afraid to cross them by myself.

Closer examination of the situation, however, changed my mind. There were several others in my class at school who were also joining the Girl Scout troop. They would be leaving school and going to the meetings too, so I would be able to walk with them. My father spoke to one of the other parents and explained my situation. Their little girl made it a point to walk with me. Out of this came not only the positive experiences of being a Girl Scout but an enduring friendship.

That experience, like so many that I had as a child, remains in the back of my mind always. Whenever I am inclined to jump to a quick conclusion about an existing situation, I think of it and force myself to take a slower, closer look.

Being realistic about the situations that confront you also means being willing to seek the counsel of others who have had similar experiences. The theory of "knowing it all" has no place here. It makes a great deal of sense to talk with someone who has already been through what you are facing, even though you know that no two experiences are exactly alike. There is enough similarity in many cases for you to alleviate your fears, strengthen your resolve, and increase your desire by talking with someone else.

This is also a useful technique for teachers, employers, and others with whom you come into contact. The modern-day term for it is "support group." But it means nothing more than a sharing of mutual experiences for the enrichment and strengthening of all those involved.

The fourth aspect is to be realistic about your future. It is the most precious gift that you have. It is your future upon which you base your goals, your hopes, and your dreams.

Being realistic about your future is not to be confused with an attitude of "I've never done this before so I'd better not try to do it now." Simply because something is new to you is no reason to avoid it, unless other factors make avoidance a good idea. For example, someone who is interested in studying computer programming and has never taken such a course of instruction should not automatically shy away from it. If, however, an aspect of working with computers is not well suited to his specific handicap, then the matter merits further consideration. Perhaps the study of computers could be undertaken with a slightly different slant. Or maybe specific aspects of computer study that are appealing to him could be found in other subject areas.

It is also important to remain open-minded about your future. Realistically, few priorities stay the same over a period of time. The very characteristics that might have made an occupation appealing to you three years ago may make it unappealing to you now. What makes you reconsider very often are the experiences you have had in the interim.

From the time I was very young my life's career ambition has been to be an attorney. I believed that my speaking and writing skills would be valuable in this profession while my visual impairment would not make this goal impossible.

That ambition has not changed, but what has been altered is the priority I am giving to it. I believe, God willing, that when the time is right I will go to law school and become the attorney that I have always wanted to be. At present, however, my need to write and share ideas about being handicapped with other people is so intense that I have put going to law school on the back burner. I believe that at the proper time this ambition will move up and occupy first place in my mind and heart.

A realistic look at your future also involves the total absence of guilt feelings concerning the course you are choosing. These guilt feelings could come from a number of sources. They can be brought about as a result of parental preferences or pressures. This involves a well-meaning parent's attempt to make you want for yourself the very thing that the parent wants for you. For example, perhaps your father is an engineer and he has always dreamed that someone in his family will follow in his footsteps. Your handicap may not preclude you from pursuing engineering as a career, and, therefore, he is eager for you to do so. You, in turn, may not have any inclinations in this area, or, even if you have, they may not be strong enough for you to make this your life's work. Guilt feelings may arise from your belief that your parents have done so much for you (they have!) that as a sort of repayment to them you should do what your father wants you to do (you shouldn't unless it's what *you* want!). When their desires and yours do not coincide, you may feel guilty that you are not fulfilling their dream for you.

Remember when this happens, however, that ultimately *you* are the one who must live your life and be happy with it. No matter how much love and support surround you from your parents, siblings, and friends, they cannot live your life for you. Their pleasure in what you are doing, however wonderful that may be, is no substitute for your own satisfaction with your work.

Guilt feelings can also arise from the impact of teachers and other adults. They too may make very well-meaning suggestions for career choices that they believe are advisable for a person with your combination of abilities and disabilities. Once again, there is no question as to the purity of their intentions, but this must not deter you from making your own ultimate choice—guilt-free. For after all, those teachers and other adults who are truly well-meaning are concerned only that you are satisfied with your choice. This means far more to them than whether or not you have followed their advice.

Your siblings and peers can also produce these guilt feelings. They may be pursuing a career that was suggested to you as providing a stable and meaningful long-term future. And well it may for the person who wants that type of job or life-style. If that is not for you, say so. Say it kindly, respectfully, but firmly. As there is truly nothing to be gained from such comparisons among siblings in the first place, you need feel no remorse at wanting to take a different path. Your choice is no better or worse than theirs. You can say only that it is better for *you!*

Out of all this should come a very real benefit: a mutual respect between you and the significant people in your life. You respect them because they sincerely have your best interest at heart. As such, they are not meddling in your life but merely trying to offer constructive suggestions to help you toward a fuller, richer future. They respect you as an individual who is concerned for his own future and who has at least some idea of the shape he wants that future to take. They also respect you as an independent thinker, as a person who is making decisions that will have an impact upon the rest of his life.

Such a mutual respect is not only healthy for you personally but also highly beneficial as preparation for future contacts with others. In your personal as well as professional life, you will be forced to deal with all types of people. Some may have a philosophy similar to yours. Other surely will not. You will be much more comfortable sharing ideas with those of varying viewpoints if you can show a respect for their ideas while still sticking to your own ideas when you remain convinced that they are right for you.

The fifth aspect is to be realistic in your relationship with God. No relationship that is to have lasting value can be based upon anything less. For any deceptions that cloud it will only cause disillusionment and frustration.

Initially, you must remember that a good relationship with God requires effort on your part. The Bible tells us that God will never forsake us, that He is always there to help His children. At the same time, however, you cannot tuck God away on a shelf in the back of your mind and bring Him out only in times of great mental or emotional stress.

Instead, realize that each day you need to set aside a time for your own conversation with God through prayer. Here, you are able to open your heart and your thoughts to Someone who will listen. You need never be afraid that you will be ridiculed or embarrassed no matter what you say to Him. Even a cry of anger or frustration at being handicapped will not incur His wrath.

The longer you practice praying, the easier and more fulfilling it will become. You know from experience with friends that they become more treasured the better you know them. Over time you learn to know them better and love them more. It is the same with God.

Also know that an abiding relationship with God will not mean smooth sailing for you from now on. Instead, it will mean that someone will always be there for you when you need Him. You cannot expect that as a God-inspired person you will find that your troubles have disappeared, that your problems have been automatically solved. To expect anything even close to that is only to set yourself up for a keen disappointment.

Many people have been known to say that knowing God does not remove problems, but it does make them easier to bear. This is so important, since we know that problems will be with us, in one form or another, all of our lives.

Your love of God will also make the good times in your life more meaningful. As with any good friend, a time shared with God is enriched to a degree that would be unheard of if you were experiencing it alone. Give freely of your good feelings to God whether that be through joy, thankfulness, or other emotions. Remember that He has an unending capacity for joy and love in much the same way as He has limitless endurance to guide you through the sorrowful times.

Whenever you are in doubt as to the extent of God's love for you, remember that He created you. A modern saying expresses it well: "God doesn't make junk." You are special to God simply because you are you.

A teacher in elementary school once gave me an A for Effort on an art assignment that she knew was particularly difficult for me due to my limited sight. By so doing, she was letting me know that while the work itself was not well done, the effort I made was highly regarded. God is much like that. He does not expect us to have the solutions to all our problems. He does expect that with His guidance we will do all that we can to work through them. He hopes that we will put our complete trust in Him.

You need only to stretch out your hand and you will find God, who is waiting to meet you with open arms. He is there for you, for me, for our loved ones. Today. Right now!

ELEVEN

Be at Peace
with Yourself

When most of us think in terms of the word peace, we think about peace among nations of the world or perhaps peace among rival factions within a nation. It is far less common to think about peace in terms of ourselves as individuals. And yet peace within yourself is vitally important to a healthy general attitude.

There are five basic elements that must be developed for you to attain this inner peace: a peaceful feeling about yourself, about your relationships with other people, about the situations that confront you in everyday living, about your future, and about your relationship with God.

Before we look at each of these elements, however, it must be pointed out that it is highly unlikely that you will possess this inner peace for long periods at a time. There are too many imponderables that can shake your sense of inner peace. "If I can't have this feeling most of the time at least, then why even bother trying to achieve it?" you ask.

The answer is very simple. Strive to achieve inner peace because of its stabilizing effect upon you. It will help you to gain a better perspective about your life, and it will afford you much-needed strength for the turbulent times you are bound to experience. Simply stated, the feeling of being at peace with yourself is like a long-awaited vacation. You sense your need to pause, regroup, and be refreshed. You know that your vacation cannot last indefinitely. Neither can your sense of inner peace. Your vacation cannot even last for as long as you like, but you still make it an important part of your yearly plans because of its therapeutic value. It is the same with striving to achieve inner peace.

The first element is a peaceful feeling about yourself. The key here is to be satisfied that you are doing all that you can at this time to shape your life the way you want it. This means taking whatever steps are necessary to add to your life those things that are now missing.

152

I experienced a keen sense of restlessness when I was nearing the end of my college education. At first, it manifested itself in a type of lethargy. I went about my daily tasks, personal as well as academic, in a mechanical fashion. My reading and study did not interest me particularly, although the subjects I was taking at the time were in my chosen major. My professors, though no less inspiring than in previous quarters, did not seem to be stimulating me as they had before. I caught myself asking, "Isn't there more to my college education than this?"

Fortunately, one of my professors sensed this and, knowing that I was normally not that type of student, forced me to examine the problem in greater depth than I would have otherwise. As we talked it over, it came out that I was really apprehensive. I was afraid that all my academic training was not preparing me well for functioning in the "real world out there."

Additionally, my parents had been involved so heavily in the world of academia that I had been exposed to little else. So much emphasis had been placed on academic achievement, in fact, that I had never really measured myself by any other yardstick.

At that time I was anything but at peace with myself. What was even more tragic was that I felt very guilty at my lack of inner peace. "I was very lucky," I kept telling myself, "to be able to go to college. I should be grateful for that and forget this lack of so-called inner peace."

Had it not been for this professor's taking a special interest, I would probably have attempted to submerge my feelings and would not have given myself the chance to find their cause. Instead, I was able to deal with them openly. "What are you really afraid of?" he wanted to know.

I had to think about that long and hard. Finally, I blurted out, "Not being able to take my lumps in the business world and not being accepted by the people in that world."

"What do you want to do about it?" he asked me without the least indication that my feelings were at all unusual.

"I don't really know," I said at first. But then I added, "I'd like to try stepping out in that world before I really have to make a decision about what I will do when I graduate. I don't know now whether to take time away from school and work awhile, and then go on to law school. Or maybe I should go directly to law school. It's all very confusing!"

After our conversation he set to work immediately and arranged an internship for me at our local chamber of commerce office, where I would be responsible for research and some media relations. This seemed like the perfect way to use my academic skills to ease into the still unfamiliar world of business.

As it turned out, the internship yielded even

greater benefits than I could ever have imagined. It not only told me much about the business world, but it also pointed up the problems that I had functioning within it. Problems like not being able to get readily from one place to another, not adapting well to the peculiarities of a clerical staff, and being ill at ease with the wide variety of projects going on all at the same time.

The first weeks were rough. I wondered whether I would make it. But the work was fascinating, and my supervisor was the most intelligent and compassionate woman I had ever met. She had a perception of what was actually going on in the world, which I admired deeply. She could adapt to almost any situation. No matter how unsettling the circumstances were, she could "roll with the punches," as she liked to put it.

I felt very much like a sponge being placed in water for the first time. There was so much to soak up. I was growing in more ways and faster than I could ever remember having grown. So I made up my mind that I would work out the problems, stick to my responsibilities, and do the very best job of which I was capable. In return, I believe that my supervisor's resolve to help me whenever possible also increased. She was well aware of my background from the very start—visual handicap and all. It was probably a challenge to her to give me the help I needed. The knowledge I gained has helped me ever since.

Thus, the truth remains that there is no substitute for facing a problem head-on even if it takes away your sense of inner peace. It may be painful to do so at the time, but it will be far less painful than allowing it to fester unattended. The path you choose will doubtless have its rocky places, but if it will help you address an area of your life that you feel needs improvement, then it is worth all the effort. For you will then be well on your way to finding the inner peace you seek.

Perhaps you are lacking in essential skills. This lack may be what is standing between you and the job you want or the goal you have set for yourself. To have a feeling of inner peace in such a case means that you should look for training opportunities—technical school, college, adult education classes, special seminars—that will help you acquire the skill you need. If your own funds are limited, it may also mean looking for ways to pay for this training. Fortunately, scholarship monies from a variety of sources are available for the dedicated student.

Perhaps your lack is not training but, rather, fewer close friends than you would like to have. Here too you must decide on a course of action to solve the problem if you are to feel at peace about yourself. This might mean becoming involved in church activities or joining a hobby club. A few hours of volunteer work each week would also be a way for you to meet new people.

Regardless of your specific lack, the important

idea to remember is that *you* must do something about it. You cannot sit idly by waiting for someone else to do it for you!

Also, remember that to be at peace with yourself does not mean that you must have all of your problems *solved*. Where would the challenge be if that were the case? And who of us could claim to be at peace with himself if we were expected to solve all our problems? What it does mean is that you must be *working toward* a solution. It may be several weeks or even months before your most troublesome problems will be solved. But you are headed in the right direction if you can honestly say to yourself, before you go to bed each night, "Today I did all that I could to work on my area of greatest personal need." Then let go of your concern until the dawn of a new day.

Always remember that God knows when you are at peace with yourself and when you are not. He is aware of every frustration, setback, and triumph you experience. Pray to Him for a sense of inner peace.

Say something like,

Dear God, I know that I am lacking in (whatever your lack may be). You know it too. This bothers me, for I want very much to do better. Guide me so that I may do all within my power to help myself. Prevent me from being so eager to solve my problem that I would take an unwise step or, worse still, hurt another person by my preoccupation with my problem. And grant me the patience, dear God, to be willing to wait for the right and perfect answer combined with the courage to act upon it when it comes. Amen.

The second element is a peaceful feeling about your relationships with other people. This element presents a greater challenge to you, because it is dependent to a degree upon the actions and reactions of others. And the extent of your control over other people is far more limited than the control you exercise over yourself. Nonetheless, you cannot truly possess inner peace if you are constantly at odds with other people.

"How do you cope with this extra variable presented by other people?" you ask. Begin by telling yourself that basically you must accept other people as they are. This does not mean, of course, that you cannot try to influence their views or alter their thinking on key issues. What it does mean is that they are not going to make *massive changes* in their personality makeup, likes or dislikes, or their manner of doing things.

As a college student I worked for a gentleman who tended to be overly protective of me. He seemed ill at ease if I left the office to run an errand or went to lunch alone or pursued any activity where he felt I might endanger myself by being alone. At first, I tried convincing him that I would attempt only those things I felt comfortable handling, but this helped the situation very little. Later I tried mentioning when I successfully completed an errand on my own. But this too had little effect. Finally, I reconciled myself to the fact that whatever his reasons, this gentleman was not going to change his attitude. It would be up to *me* to make the best of it.

I began making adjustments in my routine, such as taking care of business-related errands *before* going into the office. This way, a brief explanation as to why I would be detained the next day was all that was needed. It was easier for him and less restrictive for me.

Be aware that not all relationships that you have with other people are of the same intensity. For example, you do not need to achieve the same depth of understanding between yourself and someone you work with only occasionally as you need with your supervisor or close associate. Similarly, you do not need to work as hard to understand a casual acquaintance as you do to understand a newfound friend. What would be sufficient understanding for a working relationship would not necessarily fulfill your need for understanding in a friendship.

Therefore, it is important to know the parameters of each of the significant relationships in your life. This is also helpful as a safeguard against your expecting too much from any one person. If you and a particular individual have contact with each other only as members of a church board, for example, you would not need to be overly concerned whether or not he understood the scope of your handicap completely. For it is not likely that you and he would be placed in a situation where such knowledge would be important. If the time did come when he needed to be apprised of specific facts concerning your handicap, you could tell him what was necessary—and nothing more.

In contrast, someone whom you value as a new-found friend may need to have a better understanding of your handicap. For the two of you are likely to meet under a variety of circumstances, and such understanding may therefore be not only valuable, but essential from a medical standpoint.

Understand that different people will respond to you differently. This is not necessarily because of something you have said or done, but may be caused by experiences they have had previously. Whatever the cause, you must be prepared to handle the different types of reactions you will receive. The more at ease you are, the easier it will be for the other people involved. In some cases your best response will be to do nothing, particularly if a comment from you would not help the situation in some way. This would be true, for example, if the other people were making clearly prejudicial comments about something or someone and you knew that they were not about to change their mind.

Do your best to find the good in other people and trust that they will try to find the same in you. Be alert to the interests that you have in common with them. Focus on these areas and you will have a good base from which to start.

Above all, remind yourself that although another person can disturb your sense of inner peace for a time, he can do so *only as long as you let him.* There is no question that other people can influence your feeling of inner peace, but there is also no doubt that you have the power to limit that influence!

One of the best tools you have for putting your relationship with another person in perspective is your own self concept. Your feelings about yourself are far more powerful than any one person's ideas about you could ever be. Use that positive self concept to restore your sense of inner peace when it is shaken by someone else! Every time your self concept is used in this way, and used effectively, it too will grow in strength. You are what you think you are and what you believe you are capable of becoming!

When someone else has temporarily shaken your sense of inner peace to its very foundation, remember too the power of prayer. Turn to God and say:

Dear God, My inner peace was really shaken clear down to its roots today. In fact, I feel like I don't have very much of it left. Someone I thought I knew well told me that (whatever took place to upset you). Help me first to control my feelings of disappointment and anger. Give me sufficient understanding to at least try to put myself in the other person's place. That won't be easy, Lord. But maybe it will let me see myself as someone else sees me. Then let me know from You what I should do to mend the fences that were broken today, Lord. I am willing to try, but I'm not sure how. Guide me every step of the way. Thank You, Lord. Amen.

The third element is a peaceful feeling about the situations that confront you. Like relationships with other people, this element is not easy to control. The situations in our lives change so quickly and often so drastically that no person, handicapped or not, can honestly say that he is at peace with his situations most all the time.

There are several guidelines that can help you, however. Remember that any situation is likely to seem overpowering when you first consider it. It seems big and unmanageable. The more you think about it at that point in time, the bigger it becomes. "How can I *possibly* handle it?" you ask yourself. Inner peace is once again absent now. Doubt and turmoil within you have taken over. There is no room for feelings of inner peace.

Try to put the matter out of your mind for a while. Think about something else. Run an errand. Go for a ride to calm yourself mentally and physically. When you come back, you will feel refreshed and better able to face the situation.

When you do turn your mind back to your troublesome situation again, break it down into smaller, bite-size parts. Consider each individually. Put them together only when you are confident that you can handle them singly.

Also remind yourself of similar situations that you have dealt with successfully in the past. The reasoning is that your ability to cope with such situations before will also enable you to do so now. This should help to bolster your confidence in yourself and thereby restore some sense of inner peace.

Feel free to discuss your misgivings about the situation with another person whom you trust. The very act of bringing these misgivings into the open might minimize their significance to you. Often it is what you keep bottled up inside yourself, what you are fearful of bringing out into the open, that creates the most turmoil within you.

If a situation is so unsettling that the above suggestions for self-help are ineffective, consider talking with your minister, psychologist, or other trained professional. They are accustomed to helping people work their way through a wide variety of problems. This expertise may be just what you need to shed new light on your own situation.

Remember most of all that God is present in

every situation from beginning to end. No matter how unsettling your circumstance may seem, He is there as your stabilizer and guide. Let Him into your heart, listen to Him, and your situation will take on a new, less threatening appearance. You will have a greater feeling of control over your problem and your reaction to it as you share it with God. And, yes, most of all, you will have a greater feeling of peace within yourself.

When your situation threatens to destroy your feeling of inner peace call upon God and say:

Lord, this situation has gotten out of hand. I am not sure that I know how to describe it— even to You. But I'll try, Lord. (Describe the situation in as much detail as you wish.) You see, Lord, I feel trapped. But I know better. I'm not trapped, not really, because I have You. I turn to You now for help. What can I do to set things right? I want to listen for Your suggestions. I will sit quietly and attune my mind and heart to You completely. Show me the way I should go. Amen.

The fourth element is a peaceful feeling about your future. Here too you may find it difficult to think in terms of inner peace when you are looking at a future that is uncertain and filled with a wide variety of possibilities—some pleasant, others difficult, a few downright scary. You may wonder how anyone achieves a peaceful outlook on his future, let alone someone who is handicapped. But people do!

After college graduation I thought my future was completely planned. I would enter law school, get my degree, and go into practice. There was only one problem—I wasn't ready to take that step from college to law school when the time came. Although I wanted very much to *be* ready, a small voice inside told me that I was not. That voice became louder and louder as the summer wore on. Finally, I knew that God was telling me to hold back, to take another path. But that was all I knew. I had planned on law school for such a long time that I had thought of nothing else. "There was no need to even think about another future," I told a friend after I made my decision, "because I thought that for me there *was* no other future."

Scary? Unsettling? You bet. For weeks I did not even know what inner peace was, let alone being able to experience it. I felt as though my life had ended. What was the use of going on? If I couldn't be a lawyer (the thought never occurred to me that maybe I could be, but not just then), then why was I here? What good would I be?

At first, not even praying helped. But that was not God's fault. It was mine. For I did a very foolish thing. I prayed all right, but I forgot to *listen*. God could have revealed His most perfect plan. I would not have known. I would not have heard a word.

I became angry. "God, aren't you listening? Don't you know I'm mixed up?" And I could just as well have added, "Don't you care?" For at that point I was almost convinced that He didn't. But then something wonderful happened. I learned of an opening at an area newspaper for a governmental affairs correspondent. They needed someone to cover everything from a county commissioner's budget hearing to the sheriff's department canine corps. "That job is tailor-made for you, Gillian," a friend noted. "Tailor-made" indeed, for the job was constantly challenging, rarely routine, and never boring.

But all this came about only after I was willing to *listen* for God's direction in my life. Very simply, it meant admitting my total confusion and turning my future over to Him lock, stock, and barrel for Him to mold as He saw fit. I had come to a dead end from which there seemed no way out. God turned that dead end into an exciting road on which I am still traveling.

Remember that as late as yesterday, today was a part of your future. When you awoke this morning, you did not know what the day held in store for you. And yet you did not bury yourself beneath the bedcovers and refuse to tackle the day. Instead, you got out of bed and made your preparations for the day ahead. Perhaps you felt a tinge of uneasiness, particularly if something formidable was about to take place for you today. But did you let that stop you? No, indeed! In fact, it may have added a dash of excitement as you thought about what the outcome of this day might be!

If you are practicing your God-centered faith, you began this morning with a prayer that may have gone something like this:

Dear God, Thank You for bringing me safely through another night as You have so many times before. I am grateful too for all the things You and I have accomplished together that have brought me where I am at this very moment. Thank You for the opportunities that will be mine today. I am excited that I have been given this day to use in the best way I can. Help me to make the most of each opportunity as You would have me do—to be of help to others, to try new things, to appreciate the little things. Above all, guide me that I may know Your will for me today. Amen.

A prayer such as this spoken sincerely can prepare you and strengthen you for whatever your future—this day, next week, next year—will hold. It gives thanks for the events of the past that you have completed with God's help. It acknowledges your appreciation of and excitement for what the future holds. And, most critical to your future, it seeks God's guidance so that you will understand His plan for you. That's a winning combination—you and God!

The fifth element is a peaceful feeling about your relationship with God. Armed with such a feeling of confidence in His love for you, there is nothing you cannot share with Him. Your life— every aspect of it, from the biggest decisions to the smallest fears—is open for His inspection, molding, guidance, and understanding. There is no substitute for this relationship. No earthly being, however beloved, can take His place. His love for you and understanding of you is never-ending.

"But I don't feel at peace with God and haven't—not for a long time, anyway," you say. "What can I do?"

To be at peace with God, you must first understand His ways. To achieve this understanding, read the Bible, devotional books, and inspirational accounts of the lives of people like you who have already developed a peaceful relationship with God.

As you read, you must also pray. Your prayers need not be long, involved, or detailed. Instead, they may be simple prayers from the heart.

Dear God, I am struggling to know You better. It isn't easy, Lord. But I am trying. I want to put my trust in You and be at peace with You. Sometimes I need to feel close to You, and yet I feel very far away. Help me, God.

Steer me aright. Increase my desire to learn about You and then to listen for Your guidance as it relates to my life. Amen.

God will hear you. And you will know that He is listening to every word you say. You will feel it inside. It is a warm feeling, a relieved feeling, as though many burdens were being lifted, one by one, from your shoulders. And that is exactly what is happening. Your problems will still be there, but now there is someone who senses your longing for answers and who is willing to help you search for those answers. Take time to listen to Him. Listen carefully!

The more you confide in God, the easier it will become. Soon it will be as natural as writing a letter to a friend or calling that same friend on the telephone. In fact, you may wonder why you deprived yourself of God's counsel for such a long time before finding your way to Him. But do not dwell on the past. Once you have asked God for His forgiveness for what you have done or failed to do, leave the past behind you. Enjoy the blessings that are yours in the present—and look toward a bright future!

TWELVE

Get On
With It!

Have you ever listened while someone attempted
to explain to you how to do something, only to
find that you understood it much better than you
ever thought possible? At that time you thought
to yourself, "I can do it! With God's help, I know
I can! I just want to get in there and try! I want
to get on with it!"

Hopefully, right now you are thinking along
this same line. Only in this case, with God's help,
what you want to "get on with" is the most important challenge of all—doing all that you can
to live your life to its fullest!

As you read each chapter in this book, you reinforced and expanded your understanding of the problems you face as a handicapped person, and the important role that God plays in solving those problems. Some of the problem areas were perhaps already familiar to you. Others may have been only vaguely familiar. And still others may not have been familiar at all.

The most important point to be made here is that you have grown in your understanding of your own handicap. You grew each time you took an illustration from the previous chapters and applied it to your own situation. You also grew each time you used the small notebook suggested to complete the steps of the self-assessment exercises contained within these pages. (You may wish to repeat these exercises at a later time, since your responses and attitudes are ever-changing. This too will be a growing experience, since it will help you to stay in touch with your feelings about the person you are and the person you are becoming.) And, finally, you learned to put God's role in your life into sharper perspective.

As you grew in the knowledge of your handicap and the problems it creates in your life, you did something else too. You freed yourself from unnecessary or overblown fears and anxieties. This is not to say that different fears and anxieties will not come upon you again. They undoubtedly will. But when they do, you will be much better prepared to handle them. And it is less likely that they will be as devastating to you. You will control the situation—the situation will not control you!

But you have achieved more than an increased knowledge about your problems as a handicapped person. In addition, you have gained suggested solutions for coping with these problems. And from these solutions you have futher developed and expanded the ones that will work best for you.

Again, the more you are willing to put these solutions into action—even in the smallest of problems—the more comfortable you will become in using them. For example, if taking a quiet ride in a car helps you to keep calm and allows you to think more clearly, then the more you become used to that solution, the more beneficial it will be for you.

Avoid saying, "This is just a small problem. I'll save my solutions for the really big problems." For if you take that approach, then when the time comes to implement those solutions, they will seem strange and uncomfortable to you. Instead, implement your solutions at every possible opportunity! Make them work for you!

As a handicapped person you are constantly facing new challenges. It would be impossible to anticipate every conceivable challenge and the appropriate solution to meet it. It is for this reason that your faith and your decision to adopt a healthy general attitude toward your life become of such great importance. Such an attitude, nurtured carefully each day, becomes as much a part of you as the color of your hair and the color of your skin.

Your healthy general attitude means an entirely new way of looking at life! It means motivating yourself to do all that you can each day to accomplish your goals. It means looking on the bright side of every situation, focusing on that which is positive, good, and helpful. It means guarding against both your own negative thoughts and those of the people who would choose to focus on what makes you different from them.

Look at the facts that make your situation what it is. Which of these facts can be changed completely or at least altered in some way? Which are permanent and must be accepted as such? What can you do to minimize the problem areas in your life and enhance the strengths that you possess? Pray and pause to listen, and the answers to these questions will become clear to you.

Finally, your healthy general attitude means possessing a feeling of inner peace. It is that quiet sense of accomplishment about what you have done coupled with a determination that you will continue to do your best in the future.

But as you resolve to take your newfound knowledge and get on with living a fulfilling life, you realize the need to develop an increasingly stronger faith. Now you are ready to go even one step further and plunge into a deeper, richer relationship with your God. For you now know that God is ever-present in your life, that He wants to do all He can to enrich your life, and that He has the power to do so!

Remember that there will still be times when you feel that your faith is weak. The loss of a loved one, a setback in your own condition, the ridicule of a coworker or other negative experience at work, will undoubtedly make you ask yourself, "Can I cope with this?"

But God is also there for you during those troubled times. He will supply you with all the strength you need. Rely on Him from this day on. Share every problem with Him. You will feel refreshed and relieved from the burden of it.

Get on with your life. Each day will be just as good as you make it. Do your best. Good luck—and God bless!

About the Author

Gillian K. Holzhauser, a law student at the Claude W. Pettit College of Law, Ohio Northern University, is legally blind. Winner of two Floyd Qualls (American Council of the Blind) Scholarship Awards, she has been staff correspondent for two Ohio newspapers and is a freelance writer for various magazines. She has traveled throughout Europe and Scandinavia as a member of the National Federation of Business and Professional Women, and has spoken with and about handicapped people. Active in community relations and governmental affairs, Ms. Holzhauser is a member of the Presbyterian Disability Concerns Caucus of the Presbyterian Church, U.S.A.